Regional Integration in East Asia

Regional Integration in East Asia

From the Viewpoint of Spatial Economics

Edited by

Masahisa Fujita

First published 2007 by
PALGRAVE MACMILLAN
Houndmills, Basingstoke, Hampshire RG21 6XS and
175 Fifth Avenue, New York, N.Y. 10010
Companies and representatives throughout the world

PALGRAVE MACMILLAN is the global academic imprint of the Palgrave Macmillan division of St. Martin's Press, LLC and of Palgrave Macmillan Ltd. Macmillan® is a registered trademark in the United States, United Kingdom and other countries. Palgrave is a registered trademark in the European Union and other countries.

ISBN 13: 978–0–230–01895–2
ISBN 10: 0–230–01895–5

This book is printed on paper suitable for recycling and made from fully managed and sustained forest sources.

A catalogue record for this book is available from the British Library.

Library of Congress Cataloging-in-Publication Data
Regional integration in East Asia : from the viewpoint of spatial economics / edited by Masahisa Fujita.
    p. cm.
    Papers from an international symposium held in Tokyo, Dec. 2, 2004.
    Includes bibliographical references and index.
    ISBN 0–230–01895–5
    1. East Asia–Economic integration–Congresses. 2. Space in economics–Congresses. I. Fujita, Masahisa.
    HC460.5.R436 2007
    337.5–dc22   2006048319

10   9   8   7   6   5   4   3   2   1
16   15   14   13   12   11   10   09   08   07

Printed and bound in Great Britain by
Antony Rowe Ltd, Chippenham and Eastbourne

Contents

List of Tables

List of Figures

Notes on the Contributors

Masahisa Fujita, President of Institute of Developing Economies, Japan External Trade Organization and Professor of Kyoto University, was born in 1943. He gained his PhD from the University of Pennsylvania in 1972 and has taught at the University of Pennsylvania and Kyoto University. He has worked for IDE-JETRO since October 2003.

Young Han Kim, Associate Professor of Department of Economics, Sungkyunkwan University, was born in 1961. He gained his PhD from Indiana University in 1997 and has taught at Kangnam University as well as Indiana University and worked for Samsung Economic Research Institute as a Chief Researcher. His research focuses on international economic: international policy coordination theory and regional integration.

Paul Krugman, Professor, Economics and International Affairs, Princeton University, was born in 1953. He gained his PhD from Massachusetts Institute of Technology (MIT) in 1977 and has taught at Yale and Stanford as well as MIT. He has written and edited many books including *The Spatial Economy* (with M. Fujita and A. Venables).

Bhanupong Nidhiprabha, Associate Professor of Faculty of Economics, Thammasat University, was born in 1954. He gained his PhD from the Johns Hopkins University in 1985 and has taught at Thammasat University. His research focuses on macroeconomics, monetary economics and international economics.

Anthony J. Venables, Chief Economist, Department for International Development, and Professor, International Economics, London School of Economics and Political Science (LSE), was born in 1953. He gained his PhD from Worcester College, Oxford University in 1984 and has taught at Oxford, Essex and Sussex as well as LSE.

Yu Yongding, Director, Institute of World Economics and Politics, Chinese Academy of Social Sciences (CASS), was born in 1948. He gained his PhD from Oxford University in 1994 and has taught at the Department of World Economics at Post-Gradate School of CASS. His research focuses on macroeconomics and international finance.

Preface

This book is an outcome of the international symposium on 'Globalization and Regional Integration: From the Viewpoint of Spatial Economics', held at the Hitotsubashi Memorial Hall in Tokyo, on 2 December 2004. The symposium was organized by the Institute of Developing Economies at the Japan External Trade Organization (JETRO), and Asahi Shimbun. Chapter 1 provides an introduction to the main theme of the symposium together with an overview of the book. Part I collects the three papers presented as keynote lectures. Each paper was revised after the symposium for publication in this book. Part II is based on the panel discussion on 'Regional Integration in East Asia: Prospects and Tasks', held in the symposium following the presentation of the three keynote lectures. Each of Chapters 5 to 7 represents the revised version of the paper that was prepared for the symposium by each panel discussant. Chapter 8 presents the summary of the panel discussion session.

The editor would like to thank Asahi Shimbun for its enthusiastic support as a cosponsor of the symposium, as well as the keynote speakers and panel discussants for making this highly successful symposium possible and for agreeing to contribute papers to this volume.

MASAHISA FUJITA

1
Globalization, Regional Integration, and Spatial Economics: An Introduction

Masahisa Fujita

Globalization and regional integration – an eternal theme

With the globalization of economic activity bringing about the expansion of markets and deepening of economic interdependency beyond state borders, a new political challenge arises: how to integrate effectively the interdependent economies into a harmonious unity through the creation of new super-state institutions? This is the theme of *globalization and integration* that has repeatedly arisen throughout the history of civilization.

According to *A Study of History* by Arnold J. Toynbee (1960), for example, the Hellenic civilization, which originated along the Aegean coasts and islands around 1100 BC was confronted with the rising pressure of over-population in many city-states from around 700 BC. After many unsuccessful alternative responses such as the disastrous Spartan response of annexing by force the neighbouring lands or the Corinthian response of colonization of overseas lands, this challenge of over-population in the Hellenic society was eventually solved successfully 'by increasing the aggregate productivity of the entire Hellenic world through an economic revolution in which subsistence farming (surrounding each city-state) was replaced by cash-crop farming and by industrial production for export in exchange for imports of staple foods and raw materials' (Toynbee, 1960: 833). This successful response to an economic challenge, however, evoked a further challenge in the political sphere: 'for the now economically interdependent Hellenic world required a political régime of law and order on an ecumenical scale. The existing régime of parochial city-state dispensations, which had fostered the rise of an autarkic agricultural economy in each isolated patch of plain, no longer provided an adequate political structure

1

for a Hellenic society whose economic structure had now come to be unitary' (ibid.). However, this challenge was not met in time, which, according to Toynbee, cut short the growth of the Hellenic civilization, leading to its eventual decline.

Turning to the last half of the twentieth century, the world economy, after having successfully restructured itself in the wake of the catastrophic ruin wrought by World War I and World War II as a consequence of global competition for world markets and resources by means of force and colonization, proceeded to carry out its rapid globalization, this time through peaceful means, primarily international trade and investment. The main engine for this new phase of globalization is the steady reduction of the *transport costs* (broadly defined) entailed in the international movement of goods and services, people, money and capital, as well as information, technology and knowledge. Such a reduction of transport costs has been realized through the incessant improvement in transport technologies and the revolutionary development of information technologies, together with the continuing efforts to lower trade barriers by means of new international measures and the establishment of institutions such as the General Agreement on Tariffs and Trade (GATT) and the World Trade Organization (WTO). This continual reduction of transport costs has been promoting the rapid growth of international trade and investment, leading to the new phase of globalization involving most countries in the world. Between 1985 and 2003, for example, world trade increased at an average annual growth rate of 7.7 per cent.[1]

Globalization of the world economy, however, has not been progressing uniformly around the world. That is to say, the recent globalization of the world economy has been accompanied by an increasing tendency toward the relative concentration of world economic activity into a few sub-global regions within which economic interdependency has been intensifying at a rate more than the global average. In other words, the continual reduction in transport costs over the past half-century has been promoting simultaneously the globalization of the world economy and its regional integration at the sub-global scale, as can be seen in the next section.

Globalization and regional integration in the past half-century

To have a bird's-eye view of where in the world the economic activity is concentrated today, let us look at the night photo of the earth taken

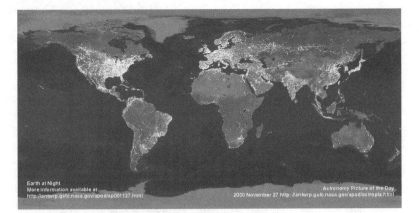

Figure 1.1 The three sparkling regions (27 November 2000) (NASA, http://visibleearth.nasa.gov/useterms.php)

from a NASA satellite (Figure 1.1). This photo shows the distribution of economic activities on the earth as the density of lights in the night.

We can readily recognize three sparkling regions (encircled in the photo), each extending across national borders. The brightest region is the core area of the NAFTA (North-American Free Trade Agreement), which contains the US together with the southern part of Canada and the northern part of Mexico. The next brightest region is Europe containing the EU (European Union). The third is East Asia extending from Japan to Indonesia along the East China Sea and South China Sea.

In fact, Figure 1.2 shows that in 2000, the three regions had roughly the same size GDP. To be precise, in 2000, the GDP of East Asia was 7,334 billion (US) dollars, which was about the same as that of EU-15 (7,926 billion dollars), while the US had the largest GDP (11,086 billion dollars).[2] Figure 1.2 also shows that over the thirty-year period from 1970 to 2000, the GDP of East Asia grew the fastest (20.7 times), while that of the EU and of NAFTA grew roughly in the same speed (EU 9.9 times and NAFTA 9.4 times).

In terms of the share in the world total GDP in 2000, East Asia yielded 23 per cent of the world GDP, EU 25 per cent, and NAFTA 35 per cent: in sum, 83 per cent of the world GDP was concentrated in the three regions. In 1980, the corresponding shares were 14 per cent for East Asia, 29 per cent for the EU, and 27 per cent for NAFTA: altogether the three regions accounted for 70 per cent. Hence, the concentration of world GDP in the three regions has been intensifying recently, with East Asia growing the fastest.

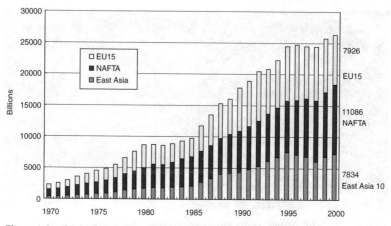

Figure 1.2   GDP of East Asia, EU15 and NAFTA (billion US dollars)

Sources: The original source is obtained from Alan Heston, Robert Summers and Bettina Aten, Penn World Table Version 6.1, Center for International Comparisons at the University of Pennsylvania (CICUP), October 2002, and converted from the PPP base to current prices by D. Hiratsuka at IDE-JETRO.

Notice in Figure 1.1 the geographical extent of the NAFTA (encircled in Figure 1.1) is about the same as that of East Asia. In fact, the flight distance between New York and Los Angeles is about the same as that between Tokyo and Bangkok. This means that, given today's transportation and information technologies, the geographical area of NAFTA or of East Asia represents a natural spatial unit of economic activity, which extends far beyond traditional nation-states though much smaller than the whole world. Notice also that East Asia contains the East China Sea and South China Sea in the middle, a geographical circumstance that renders transport cost for cargo cheaper in East Asia than in NAFTA. Thus, East Asia is not as big as is commonly thought. In contrast, the geographical extent of the EU (even the expanded 25-country configuration) is considerably smaller than that of NAFTA and of East Asia. This suggests the possibility of further expansion of the EU in the future.

Incidentally, the fast growth of the GDP of East Asia, as a whole, does not necessarily mean that economic integration in East Asia has been proceeding as well. The question is whether the economic interdependency within East Asia has been growing stronger in relation to its growth. An appropriate measure for examining this question is the *intra-regional trade share*, which represents the share of international trade (export plus import) within the region over the total trade by all countries in that region with all countries in the world. Figure 1.3 shows the change in the intra-regional trade share of each region from 1980 to 2003.

It is apparent from Figure 1.3 that among the three regions, the intra-regional trade share is the highest in the EU15, hovering around 60 per cent. This is not surprising, for many neighbouring rich countries with small lands have been cooperating in unison over the past half-century, making regional integration considerably deeper and wider. In contrast, in 1980, both East Asia and NAFTA had a much lower value of intra-trade share (34.9 per cent and 33.2 per cent, respectively) than the EU15. Since then, however, the intra-trade shares of both regions have been increasing roughly in parallel until recently. In particular, except during the period of the Asian financial crisis in 1997 and 1998, the intra-trade share of East Asia has been increasing steadily, approaching that of EU15 while becoming significantly higher than that of NAFTA. Notice also that since 1998 and thereabout, the intra-trade share of both EU15 and NAFTA has been decreasing slowly, while that of East Asia has been increasing rapidly. This partly reflects the rapid growth of East Asia, most particularly of China.[3]

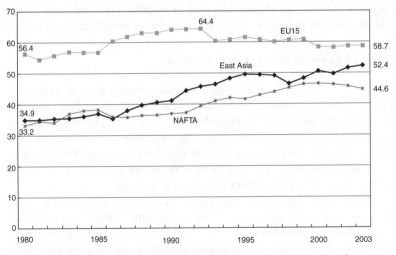

Figure 1.3 The intra-regional trade share (export + import) of each region, 1980–2003

Note: East Asia consists of ASEAN10, China, Japan, Hong Kong, South Korea, and Taiwan.
Sources: United Nation, Comtrade for EU15 and NAFTA, IMF *Direction of Trade, 2004*, CD-ROM, and Council for Economic Planning and Development, Republic of China, *Taiwan Statistical Data Book, 2004* for Taiwan. (The figure was composed by D. Hiratsuka at IDE-JETRO.)

These three figures together indicate that, over the past half-century, global economic activity (in terms of the size of GDP) has been increasingly intensifying and converging within and around each of the three regions (i.e., East Asia, EU and NAFTA), while strengthening the economic interdependency within each region. In particular, it is surprising that, unlike the EU and NAFTA, East Asia has attained such a high level of economic integration mainly through market mechanisms, with little support from region-wide political institutions.

Common sense indicates that lower transport costs would make geographical accessibility or distance less important, leading to a more even distribution of economic activity in the world. As we have seen above, however, the reality is almost the contrary. More accurately, the reduction of transport costs over the past half-century has resulted in the relative concentration of the world GDP upon the three regions, while the economic interdependency within each region is becoming stronger.

In this book, we attempt to understand this paradoxical phenomenon by using the recently developed discipline of *spatial economics*. More generally, the purpose of this book is to try to understand from the standpoint of spatial economics the recent dynamism of the global economy, with particular focus on East Asia. In addition, we will examine the prospects of regional integration in East Asia and its essential role and tasks in the future. We now proceed to clarify the meaning of spatial economics.

Spatial economics – an introduction

In this section, we give a brief history of the development of *spatial economics* as well as its basic framework. Spatial economics is often called the *new economic geography*.[4] In order to emphasize that here we are mainly concerned with the recent development of spatial economics (which aims to explain the formation of a large variety of economic agglomeration in geographical space by using a general equilibrium framework), in the rest of this section we use the term *new economic geography*.

In Chapter 2 of this book, Paul Krugman clearly explains the essence of the new economic geography, with a focus on empirical application. Thus, readers whose main interest is in the application of the new economic geography may skip the more formal presentation in the rest of this section.

The birth of the new economic geography

Until very recently, we had three distinct fields of economics, each dealing with the spatial aspects of human activity. These were: *urban economics*, which focuses on cities; *regional economics*, which, as its name implies, is the study of the so-called regions, and *international trade theory*, which concentrates on international industrial-specialization and trade. However, with the rapid development towards the borderless global economy over the past two decades, it has become increasingly clear that none of the traditional theories of urban economics, regional economics or international trade would prove adequate or appropriate for the study of the dynamics of the spatial economies taking place recently in almost all parts of the world.

For example, given the formation of the EU in 1993, an obvious question of interest was, and still is, what will be the new economic geography of the EU? For that matter, what will be the new economic geography of the expanded EU containing 25 countries? As market integration dissolves economic barriers between nations, it is apparent that traditional international trade theory, which depended crucially on the concept of national boundaries, does not provide an appropriate framework for the analysis of such questions. Furthermore, traditional urban economics had been treating cities as floating islands, unable to deal with the issues involving the location of cities, which are crucially important for the study of the borderless EU. Furthermore, the concept of 'regions' used in traditional regional economics is quite vague, at best.

Given such a problem of economics involving economic geography or the location of economic activity, a strong demand arose in the late 1980s for a new, more general theory of spatial economics, which would be appropriate for the study of an increasingly borderless world economy. As Professor Paul Samuelson once noted, 'wherever there is demand, there will be supply.'

Indeed, as is well-known, since about 1990 there has been a renaissance of theoretical and empirical work on economic geography. Among others, the pioneering work of Paul Krugman (1991a, 1991b) on the core–periphery model has triggered a new flow of interesting contributions to economic geography or spatial economics. Following this pioneering model, Anthony J. Venables and Paul Krugman together developed several interesting models of international trade and industrial agglomeration/specialization, while Paul Krugman and Masahisa Fujita worked together on the evolution of cities and urban systems. At the same time, an increasing number of young economists all over the world joined in the efforts of developing a new approach for the study of economic geography.

The work represented by this new school of economist is called *the new economic geography*, which has quickly emerged as one of the most exciting areas of contemporary economics. A comprehensive manifestation of this approach is seen in the book, *The Spatial Economy: Cities, Regions and International Trade* (1999, MIT Press), authored by Fujita, Krugman and Venables.[5] The new economic geography is expected to play a major role in economic analyses of the increasingly borderless global economy.

The basic framework of the new economic geography

The defining issue of the new economic geography is how to explain the formation of a large variety of economic agglomeration (or concentration) in geographical space. Agglomeration or the clustering of economic activity occurs at many geographical levels, having a variety of compositions. For example, one type of agglomeration arises when small shops and restaurants are clustered in a neighbourhood. Other types of agglomeration can be found in the formation of cities, all having different sizes, ranging from Tokyo with 30 million population, to Bangkok with about 6 million population, to countless small ones. Other types of agglomeration can be seen in the emergence of a variety of industrial districts such as the concentration of electronics industry in the famous Silicon Valley in the US as well as in Kuala Lumpur in Malaysia. Furthermore, spatial agglomeration in a greater geographical scale is manifested in the existence of strong regional disparities within each country. At the other extreme of the spectrum lies the core–periphery structure of the global economy corresponding to the North–South dualism. It is also important to notice that all these different types of agglomeration at different levels are embedded in a larger economy, together forming a complex system.

The traditional theory of international trade and regional economics provides a useful framework to explain the dispersion of economic activity based on factor price differentials. However, it cannot explain the agglomeration of economic activity in a borderless economy. If we use an analogy in terms of geology, the traditional trade theory provides a useful framework to explain how mountains will become flatter and flatter through erosion by water flowing from the top to the bottom, namely, the convergence process. But it does not explain why we have mountains in the first place. Table 1.1 contrasts the framework of this new school with that of the traditional (neoclassical) international/regional economics.

The hallmark of the new economic geography is the presentation of a unified approach to modelling a spatial economy characterized by a large variety of economic agglomeration, one that emphasizes the three-

Table 1.1 Contrasting the two theoretical frameworks

Traditional international/ regional economics	New economic geography
Constant returns	Increasing returns
Perfect competition	Imperfect competition
Uneven distribution of resources (first nature)	Endogenous agglomeration forces (second nature)
Borders	Transport costs
Static/long-run equilibrium	Self-organization/evolutionary

way interaction among increasing returns, transport costs (broadly defined), and the movement of productive factors, in which a general equilibrium model is combined with nonlinear dynamics and an evolutionary approach for equilibrium selection. Figure 1.4 represents the basic conceptual framework of the new economic geography.

The observed spatial configuration of economic activities is considered to be the outcome of a process involving two opposing types of forces, that is, *agglomeration* (or *centripetal*) *forces* and *dispersion* (or *centrifugal*) *forces*. As a complicated balance of these two opposing forces, a variety of local agglomeration of economic activity emerges, and the spatial structure of the entire economy is self-organized. With the gradual changes in technological and socioeconomic environments, the spatial system of the economy experiences a sequence of structural changes, evolving toward an increasingly complex system.

The formation of endogenous agglomeration forces

In this framework, then, the first two questions of obvious importance are:

1. How can we explain the agglomeration forces?
2. How can we explain the dispersion forces?

As explained previously, the answer to Question 2 is rather easy, for the concentration of economic activities at a location will naturally increase factor prices (such as land price and wage rate) and induce congestion effects (such as traffic congestion and air pollution), which can be readily explained by traditional economic theory. Thus, the principal concern of the new economic geography is Question 1, i.e.,

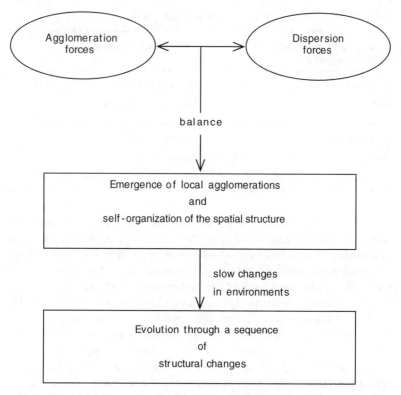

Figure 1.4   The basic framework of the new economic geography

how to explain the agglomeration forces behind the formation of a large variety of spatial agglomeration such as cities and industrial districts. Figure 1.5 presents the general principle that lies behind the economic mechanism leading to the formation of agglomeration forces.

This figure represents the idea that under the presence of a sufficient heterogeneity (i.e., differentiation) in goods (including services) or workers, the three-way interaction among increasing returns (at the individual firm level), transport costs (broadly defined), and migration of workers (= consumers) creates a circular causation leading to the agglomeration of both consumers (or users) and suppliers of these goods or services. Here, the first key element is the *heterogeneity* in goods; when goods are sufficiently differentiated from each other, their suppliers can locate in proximity without involving severe price competition, while consumers (or users) can enjoy the complementarity of such heterogeneous goods by locating close to their suppliers. The

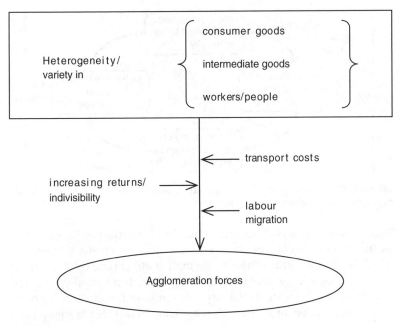

Figure 1.5 Generation of agglomeration forces

second key element is the *increasing returns* at the firm level and the indivisibility of human being. In fact, without scale economies at the firm level, there is no need to concentrate the production of each good at the same location. That is, without scale economies, the economy will degenerate into '*backyard capitalism*' in which each household or small group produces most items itself. The third key element is *transport costs*. Indeed, without transport costs (broadly defined), 'location' does not matter. In reality, the presence of transport costs yield the 'home market effect' for the suppliers locating near a large market. Finally, the *migration of workers* (= consumers) is a prerequisite for the agglomeration of workers and firms together.

Focusing on the heterogeneity in consumer goods, Figure 1.6 elaborates the circular causation leading to the agglomeration of producers of goods and their consumers into a city. Starting with the bottom box, for example, suppose that a large variety of consumer goods is produced in a city. Then, because of the transport costs, this variety of goods can be purchased at lower prices there in comparison with more distant places. Thus, given a nominal wage in the city, because of tastes for variety, the real income of workers rise in the city. This, in turn,

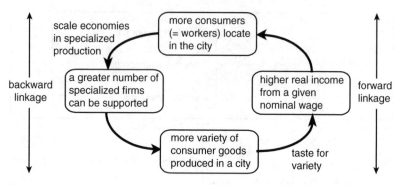

Figure 1.6 Circular causality in spatial agglomeration of consumer-goods producers and workers (= consumers)

induces more workers to migrate to the city. Then, the resulting increase in the number of consumers (= workers) creates a greater demand for goods in the city. Due to the home market effect (i.e., the benefits of locating near a large market) then, even more firms supplying a new variety of goods locate in the city. This implies the availability of an even greater variety of goods in the city. Thus, as depicted in Figure 1.6, a *circular causation* of the agglomeration of firms and workers in the city is created through *forward linkages* (the supply of a greater variety of goods increases the workers' real income) and *backward linkages* (a greater number of consumers attract more firms). That is, through the *pecuniary externalities* caused by these linkage effects, scale economies at the individual firm level are transformed into increasing returns at the level of the city as a whole.

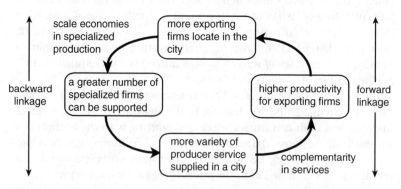

Figure 1.7 Circular causality in spatial agglomeration of final-good producers (= exporting firms) and producer-services

Likewise, taking producer-services as an example of intermediate goods, Figure 1.7 explains the agglomeration of final-good producers and the suppliers of a large variety of producer services in a city. Such an agglomeration force due to product variety in producer services (more generally, intermediate goods) can partly explain a concentration of high-technology firms or machine industries (e.g., Silicon Valley and Toyota City) or business firms (e.g., New York, Tokyo and Hong Kong).

Finally, focusing on the diversity of people/brain-workers, Figure 1.8 depicts the circular causation leading to the agglomeration of innovation activity (broadly defined) and diverse workers/people. Starting with the bottom box, agglomeration of heterogeneous people/brain-workers (together with supporting institutions and services) in a city leads to a higher productivity in innovation activity in the city through the complementarity of heterogeneous brain-workers in innovation activity (*forward linkages*). This, in turn, induces more innovation activities/institutions to agglomerate in the city. Then, the resulting increase in innovation activities creates a demand for even greater variety of brain-workers and supporting institutions in the city, leading to even more agglomeration of heterogeneous people/brain-workers (*backward linkages*). Through such a circular process of the agglomeration of heterogeneous brain-workers and innovation activities, the city accumulates the so called *tacit knowledge*, mainly through face-to-face communications among brain-workers. The local externalities form the accumulation of tacit knowledge provide the city with a further competitive advantage in innovation activity.

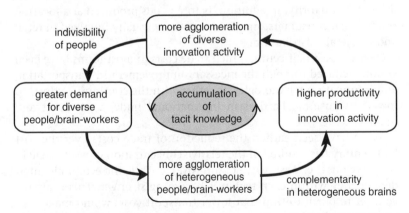

Figure 1.8 Circular causality in spatial agglomeration of innovation activity and brain-workers

In Figures 1.6 to 1.8, we have considered separately the diversity of consumer goods and intermediate goods and the heterogeneity of people as the basic source of endogenous agglomeration forces. In reality, of course, the three types of agglomeration forces work together to make industrial clusters and cities grow while interacting with the rest of the economy.

Impact of decreasing transport costs

As noted earlier, the main engine for the current new phase of globalization is the steady reduction of *transport costs* (broadly defined). In order to facilitate our understanding of what has been happening recently in connection with globalization and regional integration, we examine here the general effects of decreasing transport costs on the spatial distribution of economic activities.

To do so, however, first we must recognize that 'transport costs' in reality refer to many different kinds of costs that are entailed in the movement of goods, services, people, money and capital, as well as information, knowledge and technology. In particular, it is important to distinguish the usual costs for the transportation of goods and persons from the costs for the transfer of information through various modes of communications. Furthermore, with regard to the international trade of goods, we must consider, in addition to the usual freight costs, many other forms of trade costs such as tariffs and non-tariff barrier costs, risk from exchange-rate variation, costs for searching and acquiring the necessary information for doing business, and costs arising from different languages and cultures, many of which are often difficult to quantify. In addition, before goods produced at a location reach actual consumers, significant costs are usually involved in retail and wholesale distribution.

Over the past half-century, such trade costs in most forms have been steadily reduced through the incessant improvement in transportation and information technologies, together with the continuing efforts to lower institutional barriers in international trade, investment and finance.

As we have seen earlier, the reduction of trade costs over the past half-century has resulted in the relative concentration of world GDP in three regions, i.e., East Asia, EU and NAFTA, while the economic interdependency within each region is becoming stronger. This is almost counter to our intuition that lower transport costs would make geographical accessibility or distance less important, leading to a more even distribution of economic activity in the world. As this example

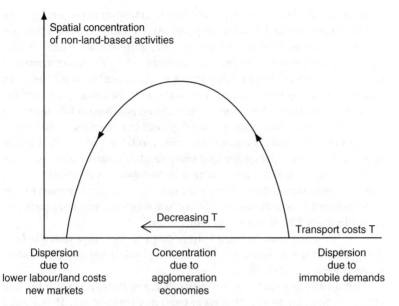

Figure 1.9   Non-monotonic impact of decreasing transport costs

indicates, in general, the impact of decreasing transport costs is complex, often involving counter-intuitive phenomena as well as non-monotonic effects. Here, with the help of Figure 1.9, let us try to understand why such complex phenomena would occur. This figure shows the general tendency in the concentration/dispersion of non-land-based activities arising from the reduction in transport costs.

To make our understanding easier, first let us consider an extreme case in which transport costs are prohibitively high. Then, since inter-regional/international trade is essentially impossible, non-land-based activities such as manufacturing and services have no choice but to disperse themselves in proportion to local demands arising from land-based activities and immobile people (due to national borders, for example), as indicated in the right-bottom part of the figure. In this case, since the economy can enjoy little scale economies or agglomeration economies, the general welfare level of the economy would be very low.

Next, suppose that transport costs decrease gradually. Then, at a certain point of time, the circular causation in spatial agglomeration of non-land-based activities (represented in Figures 1.6 to 1.8) starts working, leading to the formation of many small cities and industrial agglomerations. With a further reduction in transport costs, among such activities concentrated in small agglomerations, those ones that produce goods or services that are relatively more differentiated (and hence, having lower price-elasticities) and/or have relatively lower transport costs tend to concentrate further into a smaller number of locations. In this way, with a gradual reduction of transport costs, as indicated in the middle part of Figure 1.9, more differentiated goods with low transport costs concentrate into an even smaller number of cities or industrial agglomerations. Thus, the economy comes to have a *hierarchical spatial structure* in which larger agglomerations provide a greater variety of goods and services. With a further reduction in transport costs, eventually the economy may have a *monopolar spatial structure* in which the most highly differentiated products with relatively low transport costs are provided from the single largest city or agglomeration.

From the discussion so far, it is important to recognize that the *large agglomeration of economic activities can emerge only when transport costs of products become sufficiently low.*

With a further reduction in transport costs, however, we must pay attention to some factors that have been neglected so far. That is, in a larger agglomeration, land price naturally becomes higher, which in turn pushes up the wage rate there through higher housing costs and higher prices of non-traded goods and services. Furthermore, in an international context, since it is difficult for people to move beyond national borders, a country with a larger agglomeration of industries results in a stronger demand for labour, leading to a higher wage rate. Therefore, as indicated in the left half of Figure 1.9, with a further reduction of transport costs, those activities that use labour (or land) intensively and have relatively low transport costs start moving to smaller agglomerations in peripheral regions/countries. In this way, with a further reduction of transport costs, many industries (or labour-intensive phases of production activities) gradually shift from the core region (or country) first to nearby peripheral regions, then to further peripheral regions. Actually, this is what happened in the 'flying geese process' of economic growth in East Asia during the second-half of the last century, as will be further explained in Chapter 4.

As we have seen above, *the impact of decreasing transport costs is non-monotonic.* This is, only with a sufficient reduction in transport costs, will agglomeration economies start dominating the dispersion force of transport costs, leading the formation of economic concentrations. However, with too much concentration of economic activities in core regions, wage rates there increase together with higher land costs, which tend to push away some of activities having high labour (or land) intensity to peripheral regions.

Now, a question arises naturally. As we have seen above, when transport costs become sufficiently low, many activities start moving away from large agglomerations (or the core) to the periphery. Then, with a further development of transport and information technologies, will large agglomerations such as major metropolises eventually disappear? That is, will the so called 'death of cities' eventually happen? In the really long-run, it might happen eventually. Thus far, however, the reality shows almost the contrary. That is, with the progress of the so-called IT revolution over the past three decades, many major metropolises in the world such as New York, San Francisco, London, Paris, Tokyo, Seoul, Beijing, Shanghai, Hong Kong and Singapore are becoming more dominant than before. Furthermore, we have seen that global economic activity (in terms of the size of GDP) has been increasingly intensifying and converging within and around each of three regions, i.e., East Asia, the EU and NAFTA.

To understand such paradoxical phenomena, it is important to realize that the recent reduction in transport costs has been accompanied by a broad range of fundamental technological innovations. In particular, the so-called IT revolution (more precisely, revolution in digital technologies based on integrated circuits) over the past three decades has contributed greatly, not only to the advancement of transport technologies in the narrow sense, but also to a very broad range of innovation in production, information processing, communications and new products. This in turn has lad to the creation of a broad range of new economic activities and industries such as global finance and management, high tech R&D, and software industries. These new activities and industries are generally more knowledge intensive than traditional ones, thus tend to agglomerate in major metropolises and advanced regions through the process depicted in Figure 1.8. Therefore, the development of transport and information technologies tend to make major metropolises and advanced regions more dominant in knowledge-intensive activities.

Finally, the advancement of transport and information technologies has contributed greatly to the rapid growth of multinational firms, leading to the major reorganization of global production system and division of labour, as discussed in the next section.

Growth of multinational firms

Over the past three decades, we have witnessed a rapid increase of multinational firms (MNFs). A MNF organizes and performs discrete activities in distinct countries, which altogether form a supply chain starting at the conception of the product and ending at its delivery. This spatial fragmentation of production aims at taking advantage of differences in technologies, factor endowments or factor prices, and market sizes across countries. It is regarded as one of the main ingredients of the process of economic globalization. In particular, as will be discussed in Chapter 4, MNFs have been playing a dominant role in the economic growth and integration of East Asia. In China in 2003, for example, 57 per cent of both exports and imports were conducted by MNFs.

A typical MNF (in manufacturing industries) keeps its strategic functions such as HQs and R&D in the home country where high-skilled workers are available, while conducting its production activities in host countries as well as possibly in the home countries. There exist two major distinct reasons for conducting production activities in host countries:

1. to take advantage of low wage rates (more generally low factor prices) in host countries; and
2. to have a better access to the markets of host countries (and their neighbouring countries).

Typically, when MNFs set up their overseas production plants in developing countries (or in developed countries), reason 1 (or reason 2) is mainly at work. However, the two reasons are not mutually exclusive. For example, when a developing country (e.g., China) has a large market, the two reasons work together in setting up production plants there. For another example, when Japanese MNFs operate production plants in Mexico (or, in Poland) while aiming at the US market (or, EU market), the two reasons are simultaneously at work.

Regardless of whether reason 1 or reason 2 is mainly at work when an MNF sets up production activities overseas, the efficient organization of the MNF becomes possible only when transport costs (for products and intermediate inputs) and communication costs (among fragmented activities) are sufficiently low. Thus, the rapid increase of MNFs in the past few decades owes much to the revolutionary development of communication and information technologies over the past half-century.

Plan of the book

Following this Introduction, the book has been organized in two parts. Part I, entitled 'Regional Integration and Spatial Economics', collects the three papers that are based on the keynote lectures given at the symposium. Chapter 2 by Paul Krugman explains the essence of spatial economics or the 'new' economic geography in plain terms,[6] with a rich set of empirical data supporting the arguments. It also serves to provide the conceptual bases for understanding the regional integration taking place in various parts of the world recently. In Chapter 3, Anthony J. Venables provides a perspective on European integration from the standpoint of the new economic geography. Specifically, utilizing the recent empirical data in Europe, the chapter examines in detail the effects of European integration on industrial location, on spatial income disparities, and on the distribution of population. In Chapter 4, Masahisa Fujita examines the dynamism of East Asian economies from the viewpoint of spatial economics. This chapter also provides a background for the panel discussion.

Part II is based on the panel discussion on the prospects and tasks of regional integration in East Asia, held in the symposium following the three keynote lectures above. Chapters 5 to 7 are revised versions of the papers prepared for the symposium by each panel discussant. In Chapter 5, Yu Yongding examines the changing pattern of economic relationship in East Asia with the focus on China, and provides the tasks and prospects of regional integration in East Asia from the viewpoint of China. Next, Chapter 6 by Young-Han Kim first discusses the major challenges of Asian regional integration from the perspective of Korea, and then examines in detail the main issues by utilizing a game-theoretic model of economic integration in the context of East Asia. In Chapter 7, Bhanupong Nidhiprabha examines the present state of regional integration in ASEAN with the focus on Thailand, and discusses the prospects of regional integration in East Asia from the viewpoint of Thailand. Chapter 8 concludes the book, with the presentation of the summary of general discussions on the prospects and tasks of regional integration in East Asia, which took place in the symposium after the presentation of the three panelist-papers above.

Notes

1. Based on IMF statistics, *Direction of Trade*, December 2004.
2. Here, the East Asia includes Japan, China, the Republic of Korea, Taiwan, Hong Kong, the Philippines, Thailand, Singapore and Malaysia.
3. With the growth of China, for example, the trade with China of each country, for example, Japan, US and Germany, tends to increase more or less proportionally. However, by definition, the growth of trade of Japan with China contributes to an increase in the *intra-trade* of East Asia, while the growth of trade of the USA (or Germany) with China results in an increase in

the *extra-trade* of NAFTA (or EU). Thus, when the economy of East Asia grows the fastest in the world, other things being the same, the intra-trade share of East Asia increases, while the intra-trade share of the rest of each region tends to decrease. (To be precise, other things being the same, the intra-trade share of the region with the lowest growth rate always decrease, whereas the intra-trade share of a region with an intermediate value of growth rate tends to decrease when the fastest-growing region has a much higher growth rate than that region and when the fastest-growing region has a more significant share of the world economy.) In reality, of course, other things are not always the same: for example, if the trade costs (broadly defined) within a region (e.g., EU) decreases more than in other regions (due to free trade agreements, for example), then the intra-trade share of that region tends to increase.

4. For a historical overview of the development of spatial economics in connection with the new economic geography, see Fujita (2005). See also Fujita and Krugman (2004) for a historical review of the development of the new economic geography, and Fujita and Mori (2005) for recent development of the new economic geography.

5. See also Fujita and Thisse (2002) and Baldwin *et al.* (2003) for more recent development in the new economic geography.

6. To be precise, the *new economic geography* represents a new approach to spatial economics initiated by Paul Krugman and others in the early 1990s, which emphasizes the general equilibrium approach to modelling spatial agglomeration of economic activities. In this book, however, we use these two terms rather interchangeably.

References

Baldwin, R., R. Forslid, P. Martin, G. Ottaviano and F. Robert-Nicoud (2003) *Economic Geography and Public Policy*, Princeton: Princeton University Press.

Fujita, M. (ed.) (2005) *Spatial Economics*, in the series of 'The International Library of Critical Writings in Economics', Cheltenham, UK: Edward Elgar.

Fujita, M. and J.-F. Thisse (2002) *Economic of Agglomeration: Cities, Industrial Location and Regional Growth*, Cambridge: Cambridge University Press.

Fujita, M. and P. Krugman (2004) 'The new economic geography: Past, present and the future', *Papers in Regional Science*, 83, 139–64.

Krugman, P. (1991a) 'Increasing returns and economic geography, *Journal of Political Economy*, 99(3), 483–99.

Krugman, P. (1991b) *Geography and Trade*, Boston, MA: MIT Press.

Fujita, M. and T. Mori (2005) 'Frontiers of the new economic geography', Working Paper No. 604, Kyoto University, Institute of Economic Research.

Toynbee, A.J. (1960) *A Study of History*, Abridgement by D. C. Somervell, London: Oxford University Press.

Part I

Regional Integration and Spatial Economics

2
The 'New' Economic Geography: Where Are We?

Paul Krugman

Importance is an eigenvector. Really. The search engine Google uses links among websites to rank sites by importance, through a seemingly circular process in which a site's importance is determined by the number of links it receives from other sites, weighted by their importance. The process bears a strong formal resemblance to the process that generates geographical concentrations of economic activity in some of the models that Masahisa Fujita, Anthony Venables, and I have worked on; in both cases what emerges is the eigenvector with the largest eigenvalue. And anyone who uses Google routinely knows that the eigenvector embodies the truth: Google is almost always right about what is important.

I mention this because Google has a new service, which lets one search scholarly work the way one searches the Web; citations play the same role that links play in regular Google. When I learned about the service, I did what any academic would do, and Googled myself. And it turns out that the work I did on economic geography is, in the judgment of the eigenvector, the most important of my scholarly career. That's good to know – especially because of the fields I have worked in, geography is my personal favorite, and the collaboration with Fujita and Venables among the most fruitful.

But where does the field stand, almost 15 years after I began working in it? Where is the 'new' economic geography today? For this book, I want to provide an overview of the state of empirical play.

Four propositions

The new economic geography began with simple, stylized models designed for tractability rather than realism; in Fujita, Krugman and

Venables we described our approach as depending on 'Dixit-Stiglitz' – a highly unrealistic but tractable model of increasing returns and imperfect competition – 'icebergs' – a highly unrealistic but tractable way to incorporate transportation costs – 'evolution' – an ad hoc but tractable way to think about dynamics – and 'the computer', because even with all this sacrifice of realism to tractability the models weren't all that tractable, and numerical examples were an essential guide to theorizing. But the specifics of the models weren't the point; what we and the many other theorists who have entered this field were really trying to do was find a way to clarify a world-view about how economic interactions over space work. That world view rested on four propositions:

1. Transportation costs, or more broadly transaction costs across distance, play a crucial role in shaping international and interregional trade. In contrast to traditional trade theory, and even traditional urban economics, we argued that distance matters.
2. The interaction of market size with increasing returns plays an important role in determining the location of production. That is, we argued that some kind of home-market effect, as opposed to localized resources or more amorphous externalities, was at least one major explanation both of differences in population density and localized specialization.
3. A cumulative process in which large markets attract production, which increases the size of markets, leads to agglomeration – and possibly to multiple equilibria. Much of the excitement surrounding the new economic geography came from its suggestion that historical accident might play a major role in shaping the location of production, and also that cities and regions might be subject to discontinuous change.
4. The same processes that shape economic geography within countries also shape international trade. We hoped, finally, to justify Ohlin's claim that international trade theory is simply international location theory – or my version from 1990, that I was like Moliere's character who was startled to learn that he had been speaking prose all his life; I thought I had learned that I had been doing economic geography all my years as a trade theorist.

It was an exciting and inspiring world view, but was it right? We now have quite a lot of empirical evidence. So let's look at the propositions.

Distance matters

One of the major areas of empirical research in international economics over the past 15 years has been the estimation of 'gravity models' of trade flows. Such models are mainly useful as a way of identifying anomalies: if you want to know whether a common currency, or a common language, or a trade agreement really increase trade and if so how much, you estimate a gravity model and look for trade in excess of what that model predicts; if you believe that restrictions deter trade, you look for trade falling short of what the model predicts.

One side result of these models, however, has been the confirmation that distance matters. Despite all the advances in transportation and communication, trade between any two countries drops off dramatically as the distance between these countries increases.

Figures 2.1, 2.2, and 2.3 offer an illustration of just how powerful distance remains as a deterrent to trade. Figure 2.1 shows the income aspect of the gravity relationship at work: it shows how US trade with EU members depends on the size of each country's GDP. GDP is measured as a share of the EU total; trade, the sum of US exports to and imports from each country, is measured as a share of total US trade with the EU. As you can see, a simple 45-degree relationship, as implied by a simple gravity model, fits pretty well. And the anomalies are, as usual, illuminating: Ireland's special role as host to US-based multinationals shows up as a big trade share given its GDP, while the roles of Rotterdam and Antwerp as Europe's first and second ports are reflected in the trade shares of the Netherlands and Belgium.

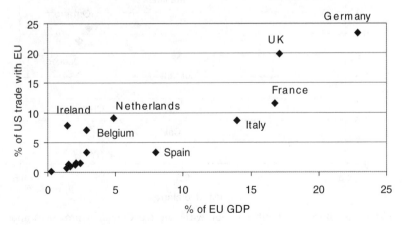

Figure 2.1   US trade with EU members

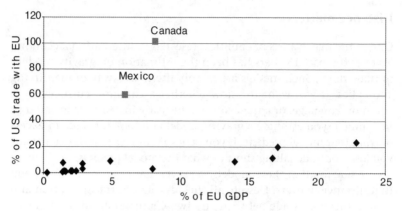

Figure 2.2   US trade with EU members, Canada and Mexico

But now take the same data, and add America's neighbours, and you get Figure 2.2. Canada and Mexico do far more trade with the US than more distant countries of equal economic size. In fact, Canada, with a Spain-sized economy only 8 per cent the size of the EU, does as much trade with the US as the whole of the EU. I can't show it here, but this outsized trade relationship predates NAFTA and the various US–Canada trade agreements; mainly, we're talking about the role of distance.

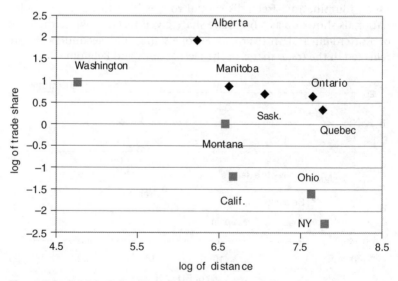

Figure 2.3   British Columbia's trade with selected Canadian provinces and selected US states

Finally, Figure 2.3 shows an illuminating set of data on the trade of the Canadian province of British Columbia. It shows BC's trade with a set of other Canadian provinces, and also with a set of US states, in each case as a share of the province or state's GDP. Within each subsample, there's a clear negative relationship. There's also a striking difference in trade within Canada and trade across the border; I'll come back to that later.

Empirical estimates of the effect of distance on trade volumes typically find an elasticity of trade with respect to distance of between –0.7 and –1. (That's consistent with the data in Figure 2.3.) It's hard to justify such a large effect in terms of literal transportation costs – so much for icebergs – leading many trade economists to talk loosely about personal contact across space. Anyway, it's clear that the role of distance in deterring trade, central to the new economic geography but ignored in most standard trade theory, is strongly confirmed by the data.

One further note: the importance of distance, and the success of gravity models, explains one of the noticeable features of recent trends in world trade: the rapid growth of trade among East Asian economies, and particularly Asian trade with China. Rapid growth in any economy is, gravity tells us, the source of rapid growth in its trade; if two economies grow fast, their mutual trade will grow very fast. And if they are relatively close geographically, their mutual trade will quickly become a major part of world trade, whether or not there are any special affinities or links.

Increasing returns and home-market effects

When production is subject to increasing returns, there is an incentive to concentrate that production in only a small number of locations. When there are transport costs, there is an incentive to choose locations that are close to large markets, and service smaller markets at long distance. Hence the home-market effect: countries and/or regions should, other things equal, tend to export goods subject to increasing returns for which they have large domestic/local demand.

It's a compelling story, but does it work in practice? Although I first wrote up that story in 1980, and it plays a crucial role in the geography work that began around 1990, until recently there wasn't much evidence that the home-market effect makes any difference in world trade. It's gratifying to note that this has changed. A growing empirical literature finds evidence that home-market effects do indeed play a role in shaping the location of production. Papers include Davis and Weinstein (1999, 2003), Feenstra et al. (1998), Hanson and Xiang (2002) and Trionfetti (2001). I won't try to summarize this literature here, except to say that it relies mainly on somewhat indirect indicators. Nonetheless, it looks as if the home-market concept has been vindicated.

Cumulative processes and multiple equilibria

The possibility of multiple equilibria, path dependence, a crucial role for history, etc. is part of what makes economic geography an exciting and appealing field. At the level of individual industrial localizations, the evidence for path dependence is overwhelming in the sense that locations are evidently arbitrary to some degree, and the historical accidents that gave rise to particular concentrations can easily be traced. But how important is the phenomenon at the level of regional or urban agglomerations?

The answer so far is that the evidence is both scarce and contradictory. I was very impressed by two recent studies that exploited the drastic events of World War II to search for evidence one way or the other. Unfortunately, they came up with opposite results.

Davis and Weinstein (2001) looked at the effects of the US bombing campaign against Japanese cities – a horrifying story, but also a natural experiment. What they found was that the extent of damage, which varied widely among cities, had no effect on a city's population once the postwar recovery was fully achieved – prewar population predicted postwar population, regardless of how severe the damage in between. As they say, this means that there is no evidence of the persistent effects of temporary shocks that we should have expected if multiple equilibria were widespread.

On the other hand, Rhode (2003) looks at the temporary US Pacific Coast boom induced by the war, and finds evidence that it kicked California and the west into a higher-level equilibrium that persisted after the war.

With only two studies along these lines, it's premature to draw large conclusions. The Davis and Weinstein results are consistent with one feature of new economic geography models that becomes apparent when one works with numerical examples: the range of multiple equilibria narrows drastically given even small natural advantages to particular locations. To the extent that Japanese cities are or were mainly in locations determined by natural harbours (or rail lines reconstructed after the war), their stability should not be too surprising.

On the other hand, it's not hard in models of regional development to get situations in which a growing region spends a substantial time with the potential for much larger population, but with that potential unrealized; that's pretty much what Rhode is suggesting. Maybe the rise of California was inevitable, but World War II accelerated its advent by a decade or two.

This needs more work; we should look for more natural experiments, though we should also hope that no more ones like the experiment exploited in these papers arise.

Interregional versus international trade

When I first began writing about geography, I made a point of emphasizing how artificial national boundaries are: any major city in the EU is closer to any other major city than NY is to LA, and Canada, as I liked to point out, is closer to the US than it is to itself. At times I came close to asserting that borders are irrelevant, and that we should think about international trade in a borderless framework. But I never did write that explicitly, and that's a good thing. For it turns out that borders still do matter, a lot.

The best evidence comes from Canada, which collects data on interprovincial trade – the basis of Figure 2.3. As you can see from the figure, Canadian provinces do much more trade with each other than they do with comparably situated US states. A rough scan of that figure suggests that the border deters trade about as much as the distance between Montana and Ohio; a number of papers have suggested that the border is, in effect, a 1,500–2,500 mile wide moat.

Why that should be the case, especially when the US–Canada border is as innocuous as a border can be (although the madness now sweeping my country may change that) is an unsettled question. But it's clear that for now, anyway, countries remain relevant economic units.

The end of distance?

We hear a great deal about globalization, and about new technologies that allow long-distance communication and trade in ways that were previously impossible. Everyone knows that the technical assistance number you call from the US or the UK may put you in touch with someone in Bangalore. But is a shrinking world changing the rules of economic geography?

Let me start by setting up a straw man. A simplistic view would be that the progress of transportation and communications technology is steadily abolishing the tyranny of distance. Once upon a time, the story would go, most economic interaction was local, with neighbouring regions or nations. Now, because air travel brings all the world within a few hours, and the Internet links everywhere instantaneously, regions 10,000 miles apart are as likely to trade as regions a few hundred miles apart.

One does hear versions of this straw man story quite often. But the facts, if anything, go the other way. Despite the evident decline in transportation and communication costs, international trade has become more localized rather than more globalized.

The most striking evidence comes from the UK; Figure 2.4 shows the direction of UK exports in 1910 and in 1996. Long-distance trade, as measured by trade not with other European nations, has diminished rather than increased in relative importance. To some extent this reflects a sharp increase in trade with Europe as a share of GDP, but non-European trade declined even as a share of GDP.

How is this possible? In a simple differentiated-products model of world trade, the type of model often used to rationalize a gravity equation, a decline in transportation costs should lead to a rise in long-distance trade and a decline in the most local trade. Obviously that model isn't good enough to fit what we actually see.

If we introduce some realistic complications into the model, however, it may be possible to make sense of the data. These complications also help us understand the difference, emphasized by Baldwin and Martin (1999), between the first wave of globalization – based on steam power and the telegraph – and the second wave, which took place after World War II and gained pace in the past 25 years.

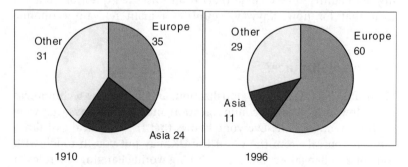

Figure 2.4   Direction of UK exports

Here's the hypothesis: in the first wave of globalization, transport costs declined enough to make large-scale trade possible – but only where there remained fairly strong comparative advantage, giving rise to substantial production cost differentials. As it happened, big comparative advantage differences tended to be associated with long distances, because regions with very different climates and land abundance from those of Western Europe tended to be a long way away from Western Europe. So long-distance trade between resource-based economies and advanced countries with a strong comparative advantage in manufacturing flourished: English machinery was traded for Indian tea, Argentine beef and Australian wool. But the costs of even local trade remained high enough to discourage intra-industry trade between countries with similar factor endowments and technological bases, even if they were close to each other.

In the second wave of globalization, transport costs have fallen low enough that small differences in products and tastes fuel trade between similar countries and regions. This meant that from the 1950s on, advanced countries began taking in each others' washing on a large scale – hence the rise both of intra-industry trade and intra-regional trade.

But it has also meant that new forms of long-distance trade have emerged. So far, the most important of these is the rise of developing-country manufacturing exports. Figure 2.5 shows the shares of manufactures and agricultural goods in developing-country exports over the past 40 years; there has been an almost complete role-reversal.

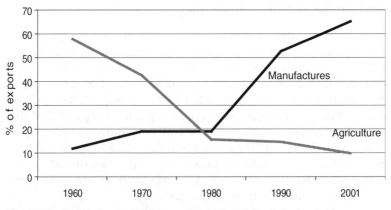

Figure 2.5 Share of manufactures and agricultural goods in developing-country exports

Long-distance trade continues to be based on strong comparative advantage, but the source of the comparative advantage of developing countries with large exports has shifted: where once it was based largely on tropical climate, now it's based largely on abundant labour. Why has this happened since the 1970s, when it didn't happen before? A best guess is that it has a lot to do with the intangible costs of making economic transactions at a distance. In 1960, wages in developing Asia were already very low compared with wages in North America or Europe, but the difficulty of coordinating production at such long distances made exporting manufactures from that region unprofitable despite that cost differential. Long-distance trade was restricted mainly to standardized commodities where the control issues mattered much less. With the falling cost of telecommunications, the fax machine, and so on, all this changed. That, at least, is the hypothesis.

The current version of this story is, of course, the rise of long-range trade in information services. It has long been possible to employ well-educated, English-speaking Indians for much less than the wages of equivalent workers in Britain or the US. Only recently, however, has it been possible to put those Indians on the other end of a 1–800 phone call.

The shift of developing-country exports toward manufactures (and now services) may be having an influence on the internal economic geography of advanced nations – one reason why agglomeration economies may be weakening.

Are centripetal forces weakening?

There are some reasons to believe that the centripetal forces empha-sized by the new economic geography – forward and backward linkages driven by the interaction of increasing returns and transport costs – actually had their peak influence some time ago, and are weakening in the twenty-first-century economy. Kim and Margo (2003), in their survey of economic geography in the US, generally seem to find that measures of regional specialization as well as disparities in income peak early in the twentieth century, if not before. This is consistent with models that suggest that declining transport costs should have a U-shaped impact on agglomeration: as costs fall, they first make agglo-meration possible, then make it unnecessary.

There may now be a globalization component to this weakening of intranational centripetal forces. Krugman and Livas-Elizonda (1996) suggested, inspired by the case of Mexico after trade liberalization, that increased access to foreign markets might weaken core–periphery patterns within developing countries. Recently Tomiura (2003) has provided evidence that increasing import penetration is weakening industrial concentration within Japan.

Where geography is taking us

A dozen years ago, it seemed to some of us that we were facing a stark choice of world visions. One vision was the traditional vision of international trade theory, in which countries are discrete economic points, whose location in space is irrelevant. Another was the pure geography vision, in which location in space is all and borders are irrelevant. Finally, there was the vision of a spaceless, borderless world in which distance had been abolished – not a world that yet exists, but possibly one just over the horizon.

What seems to have emerged from the empirical work of the past dozen years is a compromise vision. Distance matters a lot, though possibly less than it did before modern telecommunications. Borders also matter a lot, though possibly less than they did before free trade agreements. The spaceless, borderless world is still a Platonic ideal, a long way from coming into existence.

The compromise vision isn't as radical as some would like. But it's a significant change from the way most of us viewed the world economy not too long ago.

References

Baldwin, R. and P. Martin (1999) 'Two waves of globalization: Superficial similarities, fundamental differences', NBER Working Paper No. 6904.

Davis, D. R. and D. E. Weinstein (1999) 'Economic geography and regional production structure: An empirical investigation', *European Economic Review*, 43: 379–407.

Davis, D. R. and D. E. Weinstein (2001) 'Bones, bombs, and break points: The geography of economic activity', NBER Working paper 8517.

Davis, D. R. and D. E. Weinstein (2003) 'Market access, economic geography and comparative advantage: An empirical assessment', *Journal of International Economics*, 59(1), 1–23.

Feenstra, R. C., J. R. Markusen and A. Rose (1998) 'Understanding the home market effect and the gravity equation: The role of differentiating goods', NBER Working Paper No. 6804.

Hanson, G. and C. Xiang (2002) 'The home market effect and bilateral trade patterns', NBER Working Paper No. w9076.

Kim, S. and R. Margo (2003) 'Historical perspectives on US economic geography', NBER Working Paper No, 9594.

Krugman, P. and R. Livas-Elizonda (1996) 'Trade policy and the third world metropolis', *Journal of Development Economics*, 49, 137–50.

Rhode, P. (2003) 'After the war boom: Reconversion on the US Pacific Coast', NBER Working Paper No. 9584.

Tomiura, E. (2003) 'Changing economic geography and vertical linkages in Japan', *Journal of the Japanese and International Economies*, 17, 561–89.

Trionfetti, F. (2001) 'Using home-biased demand to test trade theories', *Weltwirtschaftliches Archiv*, 137(3), 404–26.

3
European Integration: A View from Spatial Economics[1]

Anthony J. Venables

Introduction

Europe's integration project has now been running for half a century. From the original six members in 1957 it has been through successive enlargements, taking it up to 25 members and 450 million people in 2004. The 1957 Treaty of Rome established the four freedoms – free mobility of goods, services, capital and labour – and these basic principles have been augmented by institution building and by the deepening of integration, most notably with the Single Market Programme of the early 1990s and by more recent monetary union. The project has been enormously successful, both in economic and political terms, although there have been frequent tensions and undoubted failures.

This chapter provides a perspective on European integration from the standpoint of economic geography. Developments in 'new economic geography' have shed light on aspects of the EU's integration experience and provided tools that may also be valuable in other integration projects, such as those in Asia and in the Americas.

Economic evaluations of European integration have posed two main questions. What are the economic gains – or losses – from integration? And how are they distributed between member countries and regions? Integration facilitates economic interactions between areas within the European Union, thus creating trade, but possibly also diverting trade that would have taken place with outside countries. As intra-union interactions increase there are changes in the attractiveness of different areas of the EU for different activities. Firms may relocate, changing labour demands, factor prices, and hence real incomes in each place. If labour is mobile then migration flows may follow, changing the distribution of population between regions and cities. Economic geography, with its cumulative causation mechanisms, suggests that these changes may potentially be quite large. The objectives of this chapter are to outline some of the changes that spatial economics suggest might occur, and to review the experience and prospects of the EU in the light of these possibilities.

Economic analysis of these issues has gone through many generations of steadily improving models. Advances have been driven by innovations of method in the academic literature, and also by the realization that analysis of the effects of deep integration among a group of similar countries requires tools different from those of traditional trade theory. The first generation approach focused on trade creation and trade diversion, raising doubts even about the presence of aggregate gains (Viner, 1950). The point is that regional integration agreements (RIAs) cause countries to specialize according to their regional comparative advantage, not their global one. For example, a country that is labour abundant relative to its RIA partners but labour scarce relative to the world but may find its production structure shifting in the 'wrong' direction. It will expand its labour-intensive sectors as it comes to export these goods to its partner countries, even though its global comparative advantage is in labour-unintensive products. However, the real income damage that this causes is typically felt not by this country, but by other countries in the RIA. Trading partners in the RIA have their imports diverted in line with intra-RIA comparative advantage, as they come to have their imports supplied by a relatively high cost partner, rather than from countries outside with RIA with global comparative advantage (Venables, 2003).

The new trade theory of the last quarter of the twentieth century focused on firms, on increasing returns to scale, and on imperfect competition. This brought a more optimistic picture of the gains from regional integration. Internal trade liberalization intensifies competition. Firms respond by merging or going bankrupt, leaving a resultant industrial structure in which average costs are lower (as remaining firms are larger and better able to exploit economies of scale) and prices are closer to marginal cost (as, even after exit or merger, the resultant market structure is more competitive). An additional mechanism touched upon in this literature (Flam, 1992) is now the subject of much current research following from the work of Melitz (2003). Firms in an industry typically have widely differing levels of technical efficiency, and those that are forced out in this process of rationalization are generally the least efficient. This amplifies the reduction in average costs associated with integration, so increasing the aggregate gains.

Increased focus on firms also brought greater attention to bear on their location decisions, and hence on the economic geography of an integrating region. If integration causes a rationalization of industrial structure, which regions are likely to gain firms, and which are likely to lose them? The first observation was that locations with good market access would tend to be relatively attractive for firms, and that this would bid up wages in these locations. The second was that ensuing high wages would attract labour inflow, increasing market size and reinforcing the market access advantage of the region. From this positive feedback the core–periphery model was born (Krugman, 1991a). The third observation was that market access derives not only from consumers' final demands but also from firms' intermediate demands, so firms producing intermediate goods tend to locate close to their downstream customers, and the downstream customers in turn want to locate close to intermediate suppliers (Venables, 1996). Clusters of industrial activity, therefore, form. Other agglomeration mechanisms – dating back to Marshall (1890) and much studied by economic geographers – reinforce this process of clustering. In all these models integration is likely to promote the spatial agglomeration of activities.

This brief review indicates how the literature now gives a rich set of tools to address the effects of economic integration on industrial location, on spatial income disparities and on the distribution of population. What do we make of the European experience of economic integration in light of this literature, and what lessons are there for other regions of the world?

Industrial location

The first issue we address is the location of firms. This not only shapes specialization and trade, but also determines factor demands and income levels in each location, and hence the incentives for population movements.

Industrial location across similar economies

Textbook international economics teaches us to expect that trade liberalization brings specialization according to comparative advantage, this typically based on technological or factor endowment differences between countries. But the core countries of the EU are quite similar in both their technological capacity and their factor endowments, and between these countries most trade is intra- rather than inter-industry. What, in this case, is the likely effect of integration on the location of industry?

One possible answer is, very little. If specialization is determined by comparative advantage and differences between countries are small then there may be some relocation, but small remaining trade frictions will mean that not much happens. However, this conclusion sits very unhappily with what we know about specialization within a large integrated region – i.e., a country such as the US or Japan. In the US there is a good deal of regional specialization, even though factor endowments are not widely different. Economic geography provides a way of reconciling these observations, by appealing to the idea of 'localization economies'. These are the economies of scale that are realized by grouping together many firms in the same industry. The sources of these economies have been discussed since (at least) Marshall (1890). They are typically grouped into three types.

The first is based on linkages between firms. Firms that supply intermediate goods want to locate close to downstream customer firms (the same market size effect as we saw in the previous sub-section) and the downstream firms want to locate close to their suppliers. In Marshall's (1890) words:

> Subsidiary trades grow up in the neighbourhood, supplying it with implements and materials, organising its traffic, and in many ways conducing to the economy of its material ... the economic use of expensive machinery can sometimes be attained in a very high degree in a district in which there is large aggregate production of the same kind ... subsidiary industries devoting themselves each to one small branch of the process of production, and working it for a great many of their neighbours, are able to keep in constant use machinery of the most highly specialised character, and to make it pay its expenses.

These ideas were the subject of a good deal of attention in the development economics literature of the 1950s and 1960s, as writers such as Myrdal (1957) and Hirschman (1958) focused on the role of backward linkages (demands from downstream firms to their suppliers) and forward linkages (supply from intermediate producers to downstream activities) in developing industrial activity. But rigorous treatment requires that the concepts are placed in an environment with increasing returns to scale, and his was done by Venables (1996), who showed how the interaction of these linkages does indeed create a positive feedback, so tending to cause clustering of activity. If linkages are primarily intra-sector then there will be clustering of firms in related activities, as described in much of the work of Porter (1990). Alternatively, if the linkages are inter-sectoral then the forces may lead to clustering of manufacturing as a whole. We return to this case in the section on income differentials.

The second of Marshall's (1890) mechanisms is based on a thick labour market:

> A localized industry gains a great advantage from the fact that it offers a constant market for skill. Employers are apt to resort to any place where they are likely to find a good choice of workers with the special skill which they require; while men seeking employment naturally go to places where there are many employers who need such skill as theirs and where therefore it is likely to find a good market. The owner of an isolated factory, even if he has good access to a plentiful supply of general labour, is often put to great shifts for want of some special skilled labour; and a skilled workman, when thrown out of employment in it, has no easy refuge.

In the modern literature this idea has surfaced in a number of forms. One is risk pooling (Krugman, 1991b), as risks associated with firm-specific shocks are pooled by a cluster of firms and workers with the same specialist skills. Another is that incentives to acquire skills are enhanced if there are many potential purchasers of such skills, avoiding the 'hold-up' problem that may arise if workers find themselves faced with a monopsony purchaser of their skills.[2]

The third mechanism is geographically concentrated technological externalities. To quote Marshall (1890) again:

> The mysteries of the trade become no mystery; but are as it were in the air ... Good work is rightly appreciated, inventions and improvements in machinery, in processes and the general organisation of the business have their merits promptly discussed; if one man starts a new idea, it is taken up by others and combined with suggestions of their own; and this it becomes the source of further new ideas.

This idea is applied in much of the regional and urban literature (see for example Henderson, 1974), as well as in some older trade literature (Ethier, 1979), and there is debate as to the extent to which these effects operate within or between sectors (as argued by Jacobs, 1969). It is perhaps best viewed as a black box for a variety of important yet difficult to model proximity benefits.

What insights do these ideas generate for the pattern of specialization within the EU? Krugman and Venables (1996) (see also Fujita et al. 1999) supposed that linkages between firms within a particular industry are stronger than linkages between firms in different industries. Placing this in a general equilibrium model with many monopolistically competitive industries, they showed how trade barriers determine location. When these barriers are very high all countries have some presence in all industries, essentially because of the need to supply final consumers in each country. However, integration lowers these barriers, allowing consumers to be supplied by imports. The clustering forces then become relatively stronger, and a process of specialization occurs. Each industry clusters in one location, benefiting from localization economies and supplying other locations through trade. Krugman and Venables showed that this creates much larger gains from integration than would be predicted by a standard model. However, it also creates substantial adjustment costs. Lots of workers have to change jobs as the specialization process takes place, and governments have to be willing to see the loss of some industries in order to specialize in others.

Notice that in this model trade costs have to fall below a threshold level before specialization occurs. It is noteworthy that, in the EU, the simple elimination of tariffs failed to produce a single integrated market, as important trade costs – such as administrative costs of crossing borders – remained. The motivation behind the EU's Single Market Programme (and to some extent also, behind monetary union) was the fact that large barriers remained in place even after several decades of customs union. Thus, to try and achieve more complete market integration, the Single Market Programme removed many border formalities, opened up sectors to competition, and deregulated some transport activities.

Industrial location in the EU

How does the actual experience of the EU line up with these theoretical arguments? The point of departure is the comparison of the EU with an area of similar size that has not had a history of trade barriers and national champions – the US. The comparison drawn by Krugman (1991b) was between the four large US regions (NE, MW, S and W) and the 4 largest countries in the EU. He showed that the industrial structures of the US regions were considerably more dissimilar from each other than were those of EU countries from each other. While it is difficult to make precise comparisons because of the inherently different sizes and geographies of the two areas, a somewhat finer comparison can be made by looking at the spatial concentration of a particular industrial sector relative to the spatial concentration of industry as a whole (the Hoover-Balassa index). Braunerhjelm *et al.* (2000) compute these measures for eight broad sectors in the US and the EU; analysis has to be at the level of these very broad sectors to be comparable. In six of the eight sectors production is more (relatively) spatially concentrated in the US than the EU, and the difference does not appear to be declining significantly through time. One of the other sectors is paper and pulp, determined largely by physical geography.

If there is less regional specialization in the EU than in the US, is there any evidence of convergence? We can address this at a finer industrial level (26 industries) by computing a measure of how different each EU country's industrial structure is from that of the rest of the EU, and tracing the evolution of this measure through time.[3] Table 3.1 reports values of the Krugman specialization index (see Krugman, 1991b) for 14 EU countries. The index takes value zero if a country has an industrial structure identical to the rest of the EU, and takes maximum value two if the country has no industries in common with the rest of the EU.

Looking first at the average (bottom row) we see a fall between 1970–73 and 1980–83, indicating that locations became more similar.

Table 3.1   Krugman specialization index

	1970–73	1980–83	1988–91	1994–97	1998–2001
Austria	0.277	**0.252**	0.271	0.309	0.351
Belgium	**0.263**	0.296	0.318	0.383	0.437
Germany	0.304	**0.294**	0.345	0.352	0.375
Denmark	**0.523**	0.550	0.579	0.569	0.575
Spain	0.386	**0.266**	0.291	0.314	0.299
Finland	0.557	**0.471**	0.511	0.596	0.687
France	**0.122**	0.123	0.156	0.159	0.175
UK	0.195	**0.169**	0.190	0.180	0.227
Greece	**0.512**	0.557	0.626	0.709	0.744
Ireland	**0.679**	0.708	0.767	0.849	0.957
Italy	**0.333**	0.361	0.360	0.429	0.481
Netherlands	**0.479**	0.543	0.536	0.512	0.511
Portugal	0.524	**0.451**	0.559	0.557	0.608
Sweden	0.396	**0.389**	0.401	0.491	0.509
Average	0.396	**0.388**	0.422	0.458	0.495

Note: Gross output, 4 year averages, 26 manufacturing sectors, row minima in bold.

But from 1980–83 onwards there has been a more or less steady increase, indicating divergence. Turning to individual countries, we see that from 1970–73 to 1980–83 seven out of fourteen countries became more specialized, while between 1980–83 and 1998–2001 all countries except the Netherlands experienced an increase in specialization. That is, they became increasingly different from the rest of the EU.

These findings suggest that a process of specialization is underway, moving the pattern of industrial specialization in the EU towards that observed in the US. However, several provisos must be made. The first is that the results above do not distinguish between specialization driven by comparative advantage and specialization driven by clustering. We know little about the relative importance of these forces. Second, the size of changes is quite small. For example, given production in the rest of the EU, Sweden's specialization index in 1998–2001 took a value of 0.509, indicating that 25 per cent of total production would have to change industry to get in line with the rest of the EU (that is 50.9 per cent divided by 2, because the measure counts positive and negative deviations for all sectors). Thus, over the near 20 year span from 1980–83 to 1998–2001 just 6 per cent of Sweden's production changed to industries out of line with the rest of Europe, a seemingly slow rate of change. And third, the results are based on analysis of 26 manufacturing sectors, and this level of aggregation may mask additional changes going on within each sector.

The pace of structural change

From the analysis of the preceding section we see that recent changes in the EU are consistent with the predictions of economic theory, as countries are becoming more specialized. However, industry was, and remains, less spatially concentrated than it is in the US, and the rate at which specialization has increased also seems to be relatively slow. What determines the pace of change, and what pointers are there to the future?

One obstacle to change is government intervention. In many EU countries there are substantial costs of plant closure, and other artificial barriers to economic reorganization remain. It is clear that some EU governments continue to resist structural change through substantial use of state aids in support of ailing national champions, although Midelfart-Knarvik and Overman (2002) argue that this has had only limited effect on the direction of specialization.

The pace of structural change also depends on sunk costs. Sunk costs of physical capital are substantial, yet seem insufficient to account for the slowness of change that we observe; there are few sectors where sunk costs are so large and capital so durable that this should support decades of persistence. More important than sunk costs of physical capital are the sunk costs of immobile human capital. These may be sector-specific skills – for example, skills in engineering or financial services – or may be firm specific. Either way, if labour is immobile, it will be a force for inertia. Sutton (2000) argues that firms are best defined in terms of their 'capabilities' and that these are typically embodied in their labour force. In some activities it is relatively easy to transfer these skills to workers in a new location by, for example, transferring a few key staff to train workers in the new location. In other activities specialist knowledge may be widely diffused between specialist workers. It may then be impossible to transfer knowledge by temporary transfer of a small number of key workers; essentially all workers would have to move. If this is not possible then the firm is locked into its existing location. We would, therefore, expect structural change, at least for the more specialist and knowledge-intensive parts of firms' activities, to be slow.

Further arguments come from the logic of agglomeration. Starting from a blank map, theory suggests that in industries prone to clustering there should be relatively few and large clusters of activity. But EU integration started from a situation where each country had its own existing industrial structure. What happens starting from a situation in which there are already clusters in place? Path dependency means that the outcome with few large clusters may not be reached. For example, suppose that agglomeration is due to cost and demand linkages, creating clusters of related industries, as in the automobile industry.[4] When trade costs are high there will be a number of clusters, for example, each EU country will have its own automobile industry. As trade barriers fall, what happens? Clustering is facilitated as the need to locate close to final consumers is reduced, and firms continue to get benefit from locating in a cluster with supplier and customer firms. However, small changes in trade barriers may produce no change in the equilibrium number of clusters; firms in a cluster derive profitability from the existence of the cluster, so are not induced to exit by marginal changes. The story is one of 'punctuated equilibrium'. Trade barriers may continue to fall for some period of time and have no effect on the spatial organization of production. A critical point is then reached at which there is discontinuous change; the old equilibrium becomes unstable and one or more of the previous clusters collapses, with production moving to remaining clusters.

This argument suggests that change may be slow. It also suggests that convergence to a comparison region (e.g. the US) may be incomplete. For any given underlying parameters of the model, there are generally multiple equilibria. For example, the equilibrium might support n, $n - 1$ or $n + 1$ clusters, all of which are stable. The actual number observed is determined by the history of the economy. It is possible to construct examples in which a country with a long history of free internal trade (the US) has just one cluster of activity in a particular sector. Another, with a history of falling trade barriers (the EU) may have lost some clusters, but still retains two or three. Even if the regions have identical parameter values (trade costs and market size) the logic of clustering, multiple equilibria and path dependence does not necessarily imply identical outcomes across the two regions. History may mean that EU countries remain less specialized.

Fragmentation, factor intensities and EU enlargement

While the early members of the EU had broadly similar factor endowment and technological capacities the same was not true for some of the later enlargements. The 'southern' enlargements of the 1980s saw the entry of Greece (1981), Spain and Portugal (1986), while the 'eastern' enlargements of 2004 have seen the entry of countries with wage rates ranging from one-quarter to one-tenth of those of the rest of the EU.

With this increased heterogeneity of EU members the scope for trade according to traditional comparative advantage is greatly increased. Recent years have seen an important new aspect of this, as it has increasingly become possible to 'fragment' production. This means that instead of producing a good as a more or less integrated production process, it is now possible to geographically separate the production of different components and assembly stages, so that goods are produced through a truly international production network.

What circumstances are required for such fragmentation of production to take place? The first element is, evidently, that there are different factor prices in different countries, so it is profitable to produce labour intensive stages of production in low wage economies, R&D intensive stages in scientist abundant countries and so on. The second requirement is that trade barriers must be low. Geographically fragmented production implies that goods – or at least, some parts of goods – cross borders multiple times, so that even quite small trade costs can create prohibitive barriers. The third requirement is that shipment of goods must be both rapid and reliable. The importance of rapid shipment is illustrated by the work of Hummels (2000). He uses US import data to estimate the costs of time in transit, and finds that these can amount to as much as 1 per cent of the value of goods shipped per day. This is far more than just interest charges on the goods, and arises in part because delay slows down the speed with which firms can react to shocks to demand or costs, thereby reducing their profitability (Harrigan and Venables, 2004). Uncertain delivery times are also disruptive to firms' activities, thereby inhibiting fragmentation.

These arguments make the point that both geography and regional integration are important to the development of this sort of trade. Proximity is required to reduce trade costs, and integration is beneficial both to reduce tariff barriers and to provide stability in the trade relations between participating nations. It is, therefore, unsurprising that there has been an explosion of this sort of trade within the EU, particularly with its new eastern neighbours. A similar thing has happened in the North American Free Trade Area, and it is likely that regional integration in Asia will magnify the already sizeable flows of this sort of trade.

Income differentials

We now turn from industrial location to the distribution of per capita income across the EU. Of course, the two issues are tightly related. The mobility of firms bids up the prices of labour and other factors, so that equilibrium income differences reflect a combination of endowment differences, technological or institutional differences, and differences arising from geography. A long-standing concern in the EU is that 'central' regions will tend to do well at the expense of 'peripheral' ones. Italian concerns about the threat integration posed to the Mezzogiorno (the poorer regions in the southern part of Italy) led to the establishment of the European Investment Bank in the 1950s with an obligation to contribute to regional development, and a regional directorate was added to the European Commission in 1974. Regional policy now amounts to over one third of European Union spending. In the next sub-section we review the theoretical arguments before turning to the EU experience in the section following.

Market access and wage gradients

In standard economic models of trade and specialization all regions gain from trade, and the expectation is of income convergence rather than divergence. However, new economic geography models point to a more complex trade-off in which, depending on the level of trade barriers, there may be forces for divergence as well as for convergence of regional incomes. The argument derives from a new economic geography model of industrial location (Fujita et al. 1999). The basic structure is a model with two sectors, one perfectly competitive (often referred to as 'agriculture') and the other monopolistically competitive containing firms that produce with increasing returns to scale and set price in excess of marginal cost ('manufacturing'). Firms engage in intra-industry trade, with each firm supplying all countries, although the presence of transport costs means that firms' sales are skewed towards their home market. The standard workhorse framework for analysing this is the model of product differentiation and monopolistic competition developed by Dixit and Stiglitz (1977), although other forms of oligopolistic interaction are possible. It is well known that in such models firms have a bias towards locating in a region that has good market access. Thus, if two regions or countries are identical except that one is $k > 1$ times larger than the other, then (given transport costs between the regions) industrial production in the larger region will exceed that in the smaller by a factor greater than k. Furthermore, this fraction will vary with the level of trade costs.

To understand the basic logic, let us call the regions 1 and 2, with 2 being k times larger than 1. Could there be an equilibrium in which firms are located in proportion to the size of the regions, so 2 has k times more manufacturing firms than 1? If transport costs are prohibitively high the answer is yes; each market is supplied only by local firms, and the number of firms is proportional to the size of the market. As trade costs are reduced, two things happen. First, the country 1 market comes to be supplied by a large number of importers, while the country 2 market is only supplied by $1/k$ as many importers, this reducing the profitability of producers in 1 relative to those in 2. Second, each firm in 2 will pay transport costs on only a small part of their output (sales to the small market in 1) while firms in 1 will pay transport costs on a larger part of their output (sales to the larger market in 2). Both arguments suggest that firms in 2 become relatively more profitable, implying that in equilibrium with free entry the number of firms in 2 must exceed the number in 1 by a factor greater than k. The large region, therefore, has a disproportionately large share of manufacturing production, and is a net exporter of manufactures and importer of agriculture.

Notice several more points about this argument. First, it holds only if transport costs lie strictly between zero and a prohibitive level. If transport costs are prohibitive no firms ship any exports; autarky production has to equal local consumption and the location of industry is in proportion to the size of the regions. Conversely, if transport costs (and all other frictions) are zero, then obviously the argument collapses, as firms in all locations have equally good access to all markets. The argument shows that it is at intermediate levels of transport costs that manufacturing is pulled disproportionately into the large region.

What are the implications for factor prices? Unless factors are in perfectly elastic supply the changes in demand for factors for use in manufacturing tends to raise factor prices in the larger country and reduce them in country 1. This is illustrated in Figure 3.1. The horizontal axis is the transport cost factor (a value of 1 corresponding to free trade, and 1.5 corresponding to transport costs equal to 50 per cent of the value of output). The left-hand vertical axis of the figure is the share of manufacturing in the large region, and the right-hand vertical axis is the real wage in the large region relative to that in the small. For the example, the large region is assumed to be three times larger then the small, $k = 3$. Labour is the only factor used in manufacturing, while the other sector of the economy ('agriculture') uses labour and a specific factor.

Figure 3.1 shows very clearly both the pull of the larger market, and the non-monotonicity of this effect. The larger location gets $k/(1 + k)$ $(= 0.75)$ of manufacturing at free trade and autarky, and its share peaks

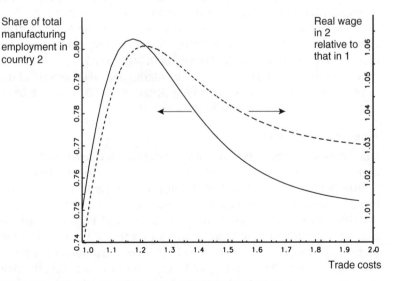

Figure 3.1 Relative manufacturing location and real wages

at transport costs of around 15 per cent. A large manufacturing presence bids up wages in the larger region, and several effects underlie the relative real wage curve in the figure (the dashed curve). Real wages in country 2 are higher than those in country 1 under autarky, because of a variety effect – the large region has more varieties on offer. At intermediate transport costs the relative real wage in country 2 is increased further because of high labour demand created by the relocation of manufacturing. As transport costs fall below the turning point, the wage gap narrows for two reasons. First, the strength of the market access effect declines. And second, as transport costs fall so the international differences in the consumer price index that are associated with transporting manufactured goods diminish. In the limit, of perfectly free trade, there is factor price equalization.

A number of remarks need to be made about this story. First, the relocation of industry is choked off by rising factor prices and, the more elastic is factor supply, the less the wage difference and the greater the relocation of industry. If several primary factors are used in manufacturing this may well amplify some factor price disparities. For example, suppose that a fraction of manufacturing costs are met by a factor in perfectly elastic supply (capital) with the remainder being labour. In this case there would be a larger relocation of industry than is illustrated in the figure, together with a larger divergence of wages, although not of firms' total costs. The quantitative impact of the changes will also be larger if clustering forces are present, a subject to which we return in the next section. Finally, all these effects will be greatly magnified by the presence of clustering forces, of the sort we outlined earlier. An established centre is an attractive place for firms to locate not just because of the size of its market, but also because of the large number of supplier or customer firms, the thick labour market, and the possibility of knowledge spillovers.

Wage gradients in the EU

One of the key stylized facts about per capita income levels in Europe – and one of the key concerns of policy makers – is the existence of a 'centre–periphery' wage gradient. As illustrated in Figure 3.2, regions of low per capita income tend to lie around the periphery of the EU, in a belt including Greece, Southern Italy, Spain and Portugal, parts of Ireland, the UK and Scandinavia, and now also the Eastern (and formerly communist) countries of the EU. A naive regression of per capita income (across NUTS2 regions[5] of 15 EU countries excluding the new entrants from Eastern Europe) on distance from Luxembourg (the

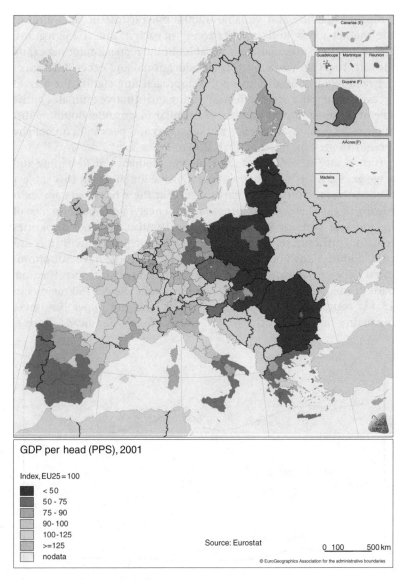

Figure 3.2 Per capita GDP (PPS), 2001, in the EU

approximate geographic centre of the EU) yields a significant negative effect, such that each doubling of distance reduces per capita income by around 15 per cent. A theory-based analysis of this relationship builds on Redding and Venables (2004) by constructing measures of the 'market access' and 'supplier access' of each of the NUTS2 regions, and using these as explanatory variables in the regression for per capita income, together with controls for educational and other differences between regions. Studies using this approach find significant market access and supplier access effects, yielding quantitative estimates of the role of distance from the centre of a similar magnitude; doubling distance reduces trade and hence market access and per capita income by around 15 per cent (see Breinlich, 2003).

Is there any evidence that these income gradients are flattening and wage gaps narrowing? There is an extensive literature on this subject that reaches the broad consensus view that there has been some narrowing of gaps between countries (as evidenced by the performance of Ireland and parts of Spain and Portugal) although large disparities remain. Furthermore, there are large spatial inequalities within countries, and in many countries (Italy, UK, Spain) these have not diminished.[6] The overall picture is given in Figure 3.3 which reports the time path of inequality in per capita income across 194 NUTS2 regions in 15 EU countries. A Theil index is used, and the upper line gives inequality between all the NUTS2 units. We see significant decline,

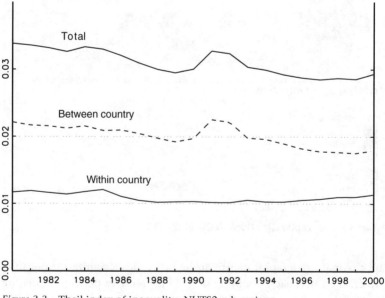

Figure 3.3   Theil index of inequality, NUTS2 sub-regions

despite an upwards blip in the early 1990s. The two lower lines decompose inequality into its between country (dashed line) and within country (lower solid line components). As is evident, between country inequality has declined much like total inequality. But within country inequality is at much the same level now as in the early 1980s, a small decline the mid-1980s being reversed in following years.

What is the bearing of geography on the spatial pattern of incomes across the EU? Table 3.2 presents some regressions that explore the determinants of the performance of different NUTS2 areas. The first two columns have as dependent variable per capita income in 1980–83. Independent variables are two simple measures of geography; distance from Luxembourg and density (population divided by area). Column 2 has fixed effects for each country, and column 1 does not. Without fixed effects we see that distance from Luxembourg has a significant negative effect – the income gradient referred to above – while density is insignificant. Adding country fixed effects means that coefficients are identified just from within country variation, and we find (column 2) that density has a positive and significant effect, while the coefficient on distance falls by a factor of three. Columns 3 and 4 repeat the same exercise for 1997–2000. Density coefficients increase in both equations, while there are very small reductions in the distance coefficients.[7]

This suggests that within-country variations in density are an important determinant of variations in per capita income. The evidence that

Table 3.2 Geography and per capita income, NUTS2

	1	2	3	4	5	6
					Growth	Growth
	Income pc	Income pc	Income pc	Income pc	rate of	rate of
	1980–83	1980–83	1997–2000	1997–2000	income pc	income pc
Density	–0.009	0.076	0.018	0.090	0.025	0.030
	(–0.43)	(5.00)	(0.94)	(6.46)	(3.18)	(3.98)
Distance Luxembourg	–0.300	–0.116	–0.290	–0.098	–0.048	–0.006
	(–8.3)	(–2.55)	(–9.04)	(–2.36)	(–3.06)	(–0.29)
Initial income pc					–0.193	–0.207
					(–7.15)	(–5.99)
Country fixed effects	no	yes	no	yes	no	yes
No. observations	194	194	194	194	194	194
R^2	0.29	0.76	0.35	0.76	0.25	0.61

Notes: All variables in logs: OLS: t-statistics in parentheses. Distance + 50km; constant term not reported. Data from OECD STAN database.

density is becoming increasingly important is confirmed in columns 5 and 6. In these columns the dependent variable is the growth in per capita income between 1980–83 and 1997–2000. Independent variables are as before, plus the level of initial income in the region; as usual, the level of initial income is significantly negative, indicating some underlying convergence. Distance from Luxembourg has negative sign, indicating that – with the other controls of the equation present – there is no evidence of the income penalty of peripherality diminishing. Most interestingly, density has a significant positive effect, so growth has tended to be faster in regions with high population densities. The final column adds country fixed effects, in order to focus on the determinants of differential growth performance within countries. The distance variable ceases to be significant, while the other two variables remain highly significant. This means that the density has an important positive effect on growth within countries, as well as between them.

Overall then, the picture painted by the spatial inequality measures and the regressions is one with the following three characteristics: (i) some process of catch up by lagging countries and regions; (ii) little evidence of the centre–periphery income gradient systematically diminishing; and (iii) sub-national inequalities due to increasing importance of variations in the density of activity increasing somewhat. Essentially, cities are doing relatively well, and it is to cities that we now turn.

The European city system

If dense city regions are doing relatively well, what implications does this have for the future economic geography of the EU? What happens if after product market integration and the adoption of the single currency, the EU achieves meaningful factor market integration? In addition to theoretical arguments, there is now a considerable body of empirical evidence pointing to the productivity enhancing effects of cities.[8] Increased labour mobility is likely to increase the extent to which agglomeration occurs, and possibly create pressure for expansion of some cities, perhaps at the expense of others. While it is very difficult to make predictions about the location of aggregate activity in a single Europe, in this section we speculate about possible developments by appealing to a well-known regularity that applies to city sizes.[9]

A feature of the urban system in many countries is that the city size distribution tends to follow the rank size rule. That is, if we rank cities

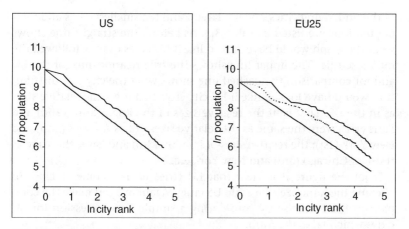

Figure 3.4   Zipf's law in the US and the EU

by size from the largest to the smallest, then the nth city has population $1/n$ that of the largest.[10] Thus, the second largest city has population one-half that of the largest, the third largest city has population one-third the largest etc. This rank size rule is illustrated in Figure 3.4, the left-hand panel of which plots the (natural) log of population against the (natural) log of the rank of city size for the top 100 US cities. Cities are ranked from largest to smallest. The highest ranked city is New York with a population of 19,876,488 in 1997.[11] The 100th largest city is Santa Barbara with a population of 198,760. The straight line, with gradient –1, shows what the graph would have looked like if US cities exactly followed the rank size rule. We can see that the US city size distribution is pretty close to obeying the rank size rule.

To make this statement more precise, we regress the log of population against the log rank of the city. For the top 100 US cities a simple OLS regression gives:

$$\ln population = 10.43 - 0.95 \ln rank$$
$$(s.e. = 0.32)$$

The 95 per cent confidence interval for the Zipf coefficient is (–0.88, 1.0) so we cannot reject the null hypothesis that Zipf's law holds.[12] The fact that the actual coefficient is less than one shows that US cities tend to be bigger than we would predict given their ranking relative to New York.

Figure 3.4 also shows the same graph for EU cities.[13] The graph is plotted for the top 96 cities in the expanded EU 25. To give some idea of the underlying cities, the ten largest and ten smallest cities and their populations are listed in Table 3.3. As before, the straight line shows what the graph would have looked like if EU cities exactly followed the rank size rule. The upper line shows the true relationship for the EU and for comparison the dashed line shows what the city size distribution would have looked like if EU city sizes had the same relative sizes as in the US. That is, if the relative sizes of the Rhein-Ruhr (2nd) and Paris (1st), were the same as the relative sizes of Los Angeles (2nd) and New York (1st); the relative sizes of London (3rd) and Paris, the same as those of Chicago (3rd) and New York etc.

From the figure it is clear that EU cities do not come as close to obeying the rank size rule as do US cities. Again, we can make the comparison more precise by considering a simple OLS regression for EU cities which takes the form:

$$\ln population = 10.05 - 0.82 \ln rank$$
$$(s.e. = 0.04)$$

The 95 per cent confidence interval for the Zipf coefficient is (−0.74, −0.9), rejecting the null hypothesis that Zipf's law holds. Notice,

Table 3.3   Largest and smallest cities in the EU 25 (top 96 cities)

Largest cities			Smallest cities		
Name	Rank	Population (thousand)	Name	Rank	Population (thousand)
Paris	1	11330.7	Grenoble	87	521.7
Rhein-Ruhr	2	11285.9	Szczecin	88	505.0
London	3	11219.0	Murcia	89	486.0
Ranstad (Netherlands)	4	6534.0	Belfast	90	484.8
			Bari	91	480.7
Madrid	5	5130.0	Montpellier	92	466.3
Milano	6	4046.7	Bratislava	93	428.8
Berlin	7	3933.3	Lublin	94	418.8
Barcelona	8	3899.2	Messina	95	415.3
Napoli	9	3612.3	Coventry	96	409.1
Manchester–Liverpool	10	3612.2			

further, that the coefficient that we estimated for the US (–0.95) does not fall within this confidence interval showing that the two coefficients are statistically significantly different from one another. As we work down the urban hierarchy in the EU, city sizes decrease much slower for the EU relative to both Zipf's law and the US. That is, the EU urban population is much more dispersed than either of these benchmark cases.

This evidence suggests that the EU city size distribution varies markedly from that found the US. Although the underlying mechanisms that drive the size distribution of cities is not well understood, the comparison obviously suggests the possibility that increased labour mobility might move the European city structure towards the outcome suggested by Zipf's law.[14] What would happen if this were to occur? And is there any evidence that such a process is underway?

Figure 3.4 already shows what would happen if Europe converged towards the US holding the size of the largest city constant around the 11 million mark. The populations of the top three cities would need to change so that the second and third city are both substantially smaller with populations of 8.9 million and 4.9 million respectively. This decline in city sizes would need to occur right across the urban hierarchy. If we take the US as an intermediate case, the smallest city we consider (Coventry) would see its population decrease from 409,100 to 229,700. Thirty-seven cities would shrink to populations below 400,000, and the total urban population in these cities would fall from 166.5 million to 102.6 million. If the distribution actually converged to the rank size rule, the second and third ranked cities would have populations around 5.7 and 3.7 million respectively, while Coventry's population would shrink to just 118,000. Sixty-seven other cities would see their population decrease below 400,000 and the total urban population more than halves to 58.3 million. Of course, these predictions of *falling* city sizes should not be taken too literally. The key point is that the *relative* size of the smaller cities will fall if the EU city size distribution converges to the rank-size rule.

Note that this example assumed that the largest city (be it Paris, Rhein-Ruhr or London) do not change in size. An alternative is to allow the size of the largest city to increase sufficiently so that the top 96 cities still accommodate the entire urban population that currently live in these cities.[15] Taking the rank size rule as a benchmark, this would require the largest city to nearly triple in size to 32.4 million. At the same time, the second largest city would increase to 16.2 million and the fourth to eighth ranked cities would also increase in size. In contrast, the third largest city would shrink slightly to 10.8 million. All remaining cities would be smaller under the benchmark than they are in the current data. A more plausible scenario emerges if we impose relative US city sizes as a benchmark. Now, the populations of the largest and second largest cities increase to 18.4 million and 14.4 million respectively. Again, the population of the third largest city shrinks somewhat to 8 million. Also, as before, other cities see their populations change. This time, the fourth to tenth ranked cities are bigger while all remaining cities see their population fall.

Evidently, this is a highly speculative exercise, but is there any evidence that such forces may have already started to operate in the EU? Table 3.4 reports the results of regressing the population growth of EU NUTS regions on their density and their density squared, together with country fixed effects to control for different rates of national population growth. While NUTS regions do not coincide with city boundaries, it is generally the case that the densest regions correspond to the largest cities, so we use density as a proxy for urban size. The first column reports results for the period 1980–82 to 1992–94 and, as is apparent, neither of the density variables have a significant impact on areas' population growth. Column 2 gives equivalent results for 1992–94 to 1999–2000, and we see that density has a negative coefficient (significant at the 10 per cent level) and density squared a pos-

Table 3.4   Population growth, EU regions

	1 NUTS2 Population growth 1980–82 to 1992–94	2 NUTS2 Population growth 1992–94 to 1999–2000	3 NUTS3 Population growth 1993–1999	4 NUTS3 Population growth 1993–1999
Density	−0.410 (−1.36)	−0.131 (−1.88)	−0.171 (−10.5)	−0.113 (−7.02)
Density squared	0.449 (0.98)	0.225 (2.13)	0.257 (8.71)	0.168 (5.53)
Country fixed effects	yes	yes	yes	no
No observations	194	194	973	973
R^2	0.11	0.21	0.19	0.05

Notes: OLS: t-statistics in parentheses. NUTS2 estimates based on density in 1980. NUTS3 based on density in 1993.

tive coefficient (significant at the 5 per cent level). This gives a predicted U-shaped relationship between density and population growth, with 189 of the observations lying on the downward sloping section, and just 5 on the upward sloping section of the predicted relationship. In other words, there is an expansion in the size of the some of the densest (and most urbanized) regions, relative to those somewhat further down the distribution. This is exactly as would be predicted if Europe's urban structure were moving towards that of the US.

The remaining two columns give results using the much larger sample of 973 NUTS3 regions. This data is only complete for a limited time period (1993–99), but the relationship estimated for this period is similar to that in column 2. Coefficients are larger and are now highly significant, and the U-shaped predicted relationship has 25 of the 973 observations lying on the upward sloping section. While columns (1) – (3) have country fixed effects to capture differences in national population growth rates, the final column omits these effects, as would be appropriate if labour were truly mobile within the EU; once again, there is evidence of a similar inverse U-shaped relationship.

These results are in line with our discussion of the possible implications of Zipf's law for the European city size distribution. There is relatively rapid growth in population for the largest (and most dense) cities, while the slowest growth – the bottom of the U-shape – occurs for the next rank of cities. As suggested in the scenarios above, urban population becomes increasingly concentrated in just a few urban areas. A number of further comments are in order. First, there are likely to be efficiency gains from this process, as productivity benefits from agglomeration are realized; of course, these may be offset by adjustment costs, and also by congestion costs unless appropriate infrastructure is put in place. Second, it is important to combine this with an understanding of what cities of different sizes do. In the US, the very largest cities tend to be reasonably diversified, while medium to smaller size cities tend to be quite specialized (see Henderson 1988, 1997 for details). This suggests an EU trend towards an outcome with some larger diversified cities and many smaller specialized cities.[16]

As we have stressed, this exercise is highly speculative. However, the discussion suggests that theory, the EU–US comparison, and recent trends in EU population movements all point to the likelihood of changes in urban structure in the direction outlined. Once again, more work is needed to think through these possibilities in greater detail.

Conclusions

Economic geography brings two important insights to economists' views of economic performance. The first is that space matters for all sorts of economic interactions. Location of industries cannot be thought of simply in terms of factor intensities and factor abundance, but also depends on transport intensity, disintegration costs and the remoteness or proximity of locations. The second is that spatially focused sources of increasing returns to scale create agglomeration forces, leading to industrial clusters and to concentration of population in cities. Both of these forces are important in shaping income disparities across regions and, in the long run, population movements.

These general messages have important implications for regional integration, both within Europe and elsewhere. The first message is that regional integration might be expected to increase diversity of economic structure between member countries. The second is that these differences in structure may be associated with differences in per capita incomes. Trade integration does not necessarily bring about factor price convergence, as the combinations of geographical advantage and agglomeration effects can bring divergence, so long as some trade frictions remain. Finally, clustering forces are likely to create 'hotspots' of economic growth. This arises as some areas – particularly large metropolitan areas – become centres of activity for the wider region. We have speculated about the form this might take in Europe, while Asia is also experiencing spectacular development of its major urban centres.

Appendix

To construct the measure of specialization we calculate the share of industry k in country i's total manufacturing output (gross production value for each industry $x_i^k(t)$) and call this variable $v_i^k(t)$. Corresponding to this, we calculate the share of the same industry in the production of all other EU countries, denoted $\bar{v}_i^k(t)$. We can then measure the difference between the industrial structure of country i and all other countries by taking the absolute values of the difference between these shares, summed over all industries:

$$K_i(t) = \Sigma_k abs\left(v_i^k(t) - \bar{v}_i^k(t)\right)$$
$$v_i^k(t) = x_i^k(t) / \sum_k x_i^k(t) \qquad\qquad \bar{v}_i^k(t) = \Sigma_{j \neq i} x_j^k(t) / \Sigma_{j \neq 1} \Sigma_k x_j^k(t)$$

This is the Krugman specialization index (see Krugman, 1991b). It takes value zero if country i has an industrial structure identical to the rest of the EU, and takes maximum value two if it has no industries in common with the rest of the EU.

Notes

1. This chapter is based on a paper prepared for 'Globalization and Regional Integration: From the viewpoint of spatial economics', Institute of Developing Economies, Japan External Trade Organization, Tokyo, 2 December 2004. Thanks to Martin Stewart and Holger Breinlich for research assistance.
2. For a recent survey see Duranton and Puga (2004).
3. This section updates findings reported in Midelfart-Knarvik et al. (2002). A higher level of sectoral aggregation is required to include data for the last period.
4. This section draws on Fujita *et al.* (1999) chapters 16 and 17.
5. Nomenclature Unites Territoriales, as reported by Eurostat (e.g., Regio database, Eurostat 1992). The NUTS2 classification divides the 15 countries of the EU (1990s) into approximately 200 areas. NUTS3 disaggregates further to approximately 1,000 areas.
6. Magrini (2004) surveys the literature on regional convergence.
7. For detailed studies of the productivity effects of density that include a wide set of controls see Ciccone and Hall(1996), Ciccone (2002), Rice and Venables (2004). The survey of Rosenthal and Strange (2004) suggests a range of estimates of the elasticity of productivity with respect to density of 0.04–0.11, compared to the estimates of 0.077–0.09 in Table 3.2.
8. See Rosenthal and Strange (2004) for a survey.
9. This section draws on Midelfart-Knarvik *et al.* (2003).
10. The rank size rule is sometimes also referred to as Zipf's Law. Zipf's law states that the distribution of city sizes follows a Pareto distribution with coefficient equal to one. Although the two concepts are used interchangeably there are important differences between them which revolve around the fact that the rank size rule is a deterministic relationship whereas Zipf's Law is probabilistic. See Gabaix and Ioannides (2003) for more details. For our speculative purposes, these differences do not matter and so we consider the more intuitive rank size rule.
11. Although we use the term 'city', data are actually for Metropolitan Statistical Areas taken from the US Bureau of the Census, State and Metropolitan Area Data Book 1997–98, Table B.1. See Cheshire (1999) for a discussion.
12. As is well known, for the US, increasing the sample size up to approximately 140 cities brings the coefficient closer to 1. Increasing from 140 to 237 cities (the number of agglomerations with population larger than 50,000) moves the coefficient back away from one. See Black and Henderson (2003) for more details.
13. Data on EU cities is taken from the world gazetteer (www.worldgazetteer.com). Data are for metropolitan areas with population greater than 400,000. Metropolitan areas may comprise several cities linked to one another economically, possibly extending across regional and national boundaries. Data comes from a variety of sources (official and unofficial)

and so is not guaranteed to be strictly comparable across countries. Results are not sensitive to the inclusion or exclusion or particular cities or to fairly large changes in terms of the size of individual cities. What matters here is that the rate of decline in city size across the entire top 100 cities is low compared to the US.

14. Gabaix (1999) and Duranton (2003) derive theoretical explanations for the emergence of Zipf's Law, driven by shocks to amenities and technology respectively.

15. The urban population for any given system can be calculated using the area under the corresponding curve shown in Figure 3.4. Our first two examples took the intercept (the size of the largest city) as given and imposed a slope (relative city sizes) consistent with the rank-size rule while allowing the area under the curve (total urban population) to change. Our second two examples hold the area (total urban population) given and allow the intecept (the size of the largest city) to change as we impose the relevant slope (relative city sizes) consistent with the rank size rule.

16. The determinants of the relative numbers of diversified and specialized cities are not well understood and the relative numbers need not be constant over time. In a recent piece Duranton and Puga (2001) suggest that the existence of the two types of cities is intimately connected to the existence of product life cycles. In the early stages of producing a product firms locate in large diversified cities while they work out the best production strategy, only moving to specialized cities later in the product life cycle. Changes in the length of product life cycles could thus change the relative numbers of diversified and specialized cities.

References

Amiti, M. (1999) 'Specialization patterns in Europe', *Weltwirtschaftliches Archiv*, 135, 1–21.

Baldwin, R. E., R. Forslid, J. I. Haaland and K. H. Midelfart-Knarvik (2001), 'EU integration and outsiders: A simulation study of industrial location', in R. E. Baldwin and A. Brunetti (eds), *Economic Impact of EU Membership on Entrants. New Methods and Issues*, Boston: Kluwer.

Black, D. and J. V. Henderson (2003) 'Spatial Evolution in the USA', *Journal of Economic Geography*, 3, 343–72.

Braunerhjelm, P., R. Faini, V. D. Norman, F. Ruane and P. Seabright (2000) 'Integration and the regions of Europe: how the right policies can prevent polarization', *Monitoring European Integration 10'*, Centre for Economic Policy Research.

Breinlich, H. (2003) *Economic Geography and the Regional Income Structure in the EU*, London: LSE, Centre for Economic Performance.

Brülhart, M. (1998a) 'Economic geography, industry location, and trade: The evidence', *The World Economy*, 21, 775–801.

Brülhart, M. (1998b) 'Trading places: Industrial specialization in the European Union', *Journal of Common Market Studies*, 36(3): 319–46.

Brülhart, M. and J. Torstensson (1996) 'Regional integration, scale economies and industry location in the European Union', CEPR Discussion Paper No. 1435.

Brülhart, M. and R. Traeger (2003) 'An account of geographic concentration patterns in Europe', processed University of Lausanne, online at: http://www.hec.unil.ch/mbrulhar/papers/rt37.pdf

Cheshire, P. (1999) 'Trends in Sizes and Structure of Urban Areas', in P. Cheshire and E. S. Mills (eds), *Handbook of Regional and Urban Economics*, vol. 3, North Holland.

Ciccone, A. (2002) 'Agglomeration effects in Europe', *European Economic Review*, 46(2), 213–28.

Ciccone, A. and R. Hall (1996) 'Productivity and the density of economic activity', *American Economic Review*, 86(1), 54–70.

Combes, P.-P. and H. G. Overman (2003) 'The spatial distribution of economic activity in the European Union', in J. V. Henderson and J.-F. Thisse (eds), *Handbook of Urban and Regional Economics*, vol. 4, North Holland.

Dixit, A. and J. E. Stiglitz (1977) 'Monopolistic completion and optimal product diversity', *American Economic Review*, 67(3), 297–308.

Duranton, G. (2003) 'City size distributions as a consequence of the growth process', processed LSE.

Duranton, G. and D. Puga (2001) 'Nursery cities: Urban diversity, process innovation, and the life-cycle of product', *American Economic Review*, 91(5), 1454–77.

Duranton, G. and D. Puga (2004) 'Micro-foundations of urban agglomeration economies', NBER Working Paper No. 9931.

Ellison, G. and E. L. Glaeser (1999) 'The geographic concentration of industry: Does natural advantage explain agglomeration?', *American Economic Review*, 89, 311–16.

Ethier, W. (1979) 'Internationally decreasing costs and world trade', *Journal of International Economics*, 9(1), 1–24.

Flam, H. (1992) 'Product markets and 1992: Full integration, large gains', *Journal of Economic Perspectives*, 6, 7–30.

Fujita, M., P. Krugman and A. J. Venables (1999) *The Spatial Economy: Cities, Regions and International Trade*, Cambridge, MA: MIT Press.

Gabaix, Z. (1999) 'Zipf's law for cities: An explanation', *Quarterly Journal of Economics*, CXIV, August, 739–67.

Gabaix, X. and Y. Ioannides (2004) 'The evolution of city size distributions', in J. V. Henderson and J. Thisse (eds), *Handbook of Urban and Regional Economics*, vol. 4, North Holland.

Hallet, M. (2000) 'Regional specialisation and concentration in the EU', European Commission, DG for Economic and Financial Affairs, Economic Papers No. 141.

Harrigan, J. and A. Venables (2004) 'Timeliness, trade and agglomeration', NBER Working Paper No. 10404.

Henderson, J. V. (1974) 'The sizes and types of cities', *American Economic Review*, 64(4), 640–56.

Henderson, J. V. (1988), *Urban Development: Theory, Fact, and Illusion*, Oxford: Oxford University Press.

Henderson, V. (1997), 'Medium size cities', *Regional Science and Urban Economics*, 27, 583–612.

Hirschman, A. (1958) *The Strategy of Economic Development*, New Haven: Yale University Press.

Hummels, D. (1999) 'Have international transportation costs declined', mimeo, Chicago.

Hummels, D. (2000) 'Time as a trade barrier', mimeo, Purdue University.

Hummels, D., J. Ishii and K.-M. Yi (2001) 'The nature and growth of vertical specialization in world trade', *Journal of International Economics*, 75–96.

Jacobs, J. (1969) *The Economy of Cities*, New York: Random House.

Krugman, P. (1991a) 'Increasing returns and economic geography', *Journal of Political Economy*, 99: 483–499.

Krugman, P. (1991b) *Geography and Trade*, Gaston Eyskens Lecture Series, Cambridge, MA, and London: MIT Press; Louvain, Belgium: Louvain University Press.

Krugman, P. and A.J. Venables (1990) 'Integration and the competitiveness of peripheral industries', in C. Bliss and C. de Macedo (eds), *Unity with Diversity in the European Community*, Cambridge: Cambridge University Press.

Krugman P. and A. J. Venables (1995) 'Globalization and the inequality of nations', *Quarterly Journal of Economics*, 110, 857–80.

Krugman P. and A. J. Venables (1996) 'Integration, specialization and adjustment', *European Economic Review*, 40, 959–67.

Magrini, S. (2004) 'Regional (di) convergence', in V. Henderson and J. Thisse (eds) *Handbook of Urban and Regional Economics*, vol. 4, North Holland.

Markusen J. R. (2002) '*Multinational Firms and the Theory of International Trade*, Cambridge, MA: MIT Press.

Markusen J. R. and A. J. Venables (2004) 'A Multi-Country Model with Multi-Stage Production and Country-Specific Trade Costs: A Generalization of Factor-Proportions Trade Theory', mimeo, Boulder, CO.

Marshall, A. (1890) *Principles of Economics*, London: Macmillan (8th edition, 1920).

Melitz, M. J. (2003) 'The impact of trade on intra-industry reallocations and aggregate industry productivity', *Econometrica*, 71, 1695–725.

Midelfart-Knarvik, K. H. and H. G. Overman (2002) 'Delocation and European integration: Is structural spending justified', *Economic Policy*, 35, 323–59.

Midelfart-Knarvik, K. H., H. G. Overman, S. J. Redding and A. J. Venables (2002) 'The location of European industry', *European Economy*, 2, 216–73 and, European Commission, DG for Economic and Financial Affairs, *Economic Papers* No. 142.

Midelfart-Knarvik, K. H, H. G. Overman and A. J. Venables (2003) 'Monetary union and the economic geography of Europe', *Journal of Common Market Studies*, 41, 847–68.

Myrdal, G. (1957) *Economic Theory and Under-Developed Regions*, London: Duckworth.

Porter, M. E. (1990) *The competitive advantage of nations*, London: Macmillan.

Puga, D. (2002) 'European regional policies in the light or recent location theories', *Journal of Economic Geography*, 4: 373–406.

Redding, S. and A. J. Venables (2004) 'Economic geography and international inequality', *Journal of International Economics*, 62, 53–82.

Rice, P. G and A. J. Venables (2004) 'Spatial determinants of productivity: Analysis for the regions of Great Britain', CEPR discussion paper No. 4527.

Rosenthal, S. S. and W. C. Strange (2004) 'Evidence on the nature and sources of agglomeration economies', in V. Henderson and J. Thisse (eds), *Handbook of Urban and Regional Economics*, vol. 4, North Holland.

Storper, M., Y. Chen and F. De Paolis (2002) 'Trade and the location of industries in the OECD and European Union', *Journal of Economic Geography*, 2(1), 73–107.

Sutton, J. (2000) 'Rich trades, scarce capabilities: Industrial development revisited', STICERD discussion paper no. EI28, LSE.

Venables, A. J. (1996) 'Equilibrium locations of vertically linked industries', *International Economic Review*, 37, 341–59.

Venables, A. J. (1999) 'Fragmentation and multinational production', *European Economic Review*, 43, 935–45.

Venables, A. J. (2003) 'Winners and losers from regional integration agreements', *Economic Journal*, 113, 747–61.

Venables, A. J. and N. Limao (2002) 'Geographical disadvantage: A Heckscher-Ohlin-von Thünen model of international specialisation', *Journal of International Economics*, 58, 239–63.

Viner, J. (1950) *The Customs Union Issue*, New York: Carnegie Endowment for International Peace.

WIFO (1999) 'Specialisation and (geographic) concentration of European manufacturing', background paper for 'The Competitiveness of European Industry: The 1999 report', EC Enterprise Directorate-General, working paper no. 1, Brussels.

4
Development of East Asian Regional Economies: A View from Spatial Economics

Masahisa Fujita

Introduction

We have seen in Chapter 1 that the recent globalization of the world economy has been accompanied by an increasing tendency toward the relative concentration of world economic activity into the three sub-global regions, i.e., East Asia, EU and NAFTA, while strengthening the economic interdependency in each region. In particular, over the past three decades, East Asia has been growing the fastest, while the strength of economic interdependency within East Asia (in terms of intra-regional trade share) is approaching that of the EU. In this chapter, we focus on East Asia, and examine more closely the dynamics of its economy over the past few decades, paving the way to the panel discussion on the prospects and tasks of East Asian regional integration in Part II.

Specifically, in the following section, we review the growth and regional integration of East Asia in terms of macro indicators such as GDP and trade. Then, we examine the evolution of regional economies and industrial development in East Asia over the past few decades. The next section examines the diversity of East Asia in terms of various regional indicators. The final section concludes this chapter with a brief discussion of the future tasks towards further promotion of regional integration in East Asia.

De facto integration of East Asia

In Chapter 1, through Figures 1.2 and 1.3, we have seen that the strength of economic interdependency within East Asia has been increasing steadily over the past three decades, while achieving the fastest economic growth in the world. In this section, we examine more closely the economic interdependency within East Asia as well as that between East Asia and the rest of the world.

First, to show more precisely the structure of economic inter-dependency within East Asia, we add two lines to Figure 1.3, and get Figure 4.1.

One of two new lines in the bottom part of Figure 4.1 shows the change in the intra-regional trade share of ASEAN-10 region from 1980 to 2003, whereas the other line shows that of the China-Japan-Korea region (North East Asia). We can see from the figure that the intra-trade share of each sub-region of East Asia is much lower than that of the entire East Asia (which consists of ASEAN 10 and China-Japan-Korea plus Taiwan and Hong Kong). For example, in 2003, the intra-trade share of ASEAN 10 was 22.2 per cent, that of China-Japan-Korea was 25.8 per cent, whereas that of East Asia was 52.4 per cent. This indicates that although neither ASEAN alone nor China-Japan-Korea alone represents a sufficiently integrated region, the two sub-regions together constitute an integrated region with a strong interdependency. We can also see from Figure 4.1 that over the past several years,

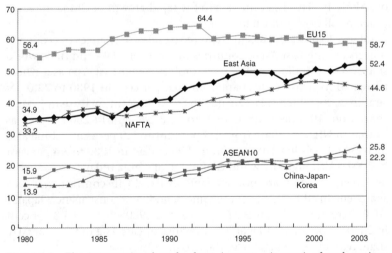

Figure 4.1 The intra-regional trade share (export + import) of each region, 1980–2003

Note: East Asia consists of ASEAN10, China, Japan, Hong Kong, South Korea and Taiwan.
Sources: United Nation, Comtrade for EU15 and NAFTA, IMF *Direction of Trade, 2004*, CD-ROM, and Council for Economic Planning and Development, Republic of China, *Taiwan Statistical Data Book, 2004* for Taiwan. (The figure was composed by D. Hiratsuka at IDE-JETRO.)

Table 4.1   Recent development of East Asia in terms of world shares in GDP and trade

		World shares in GDP and trade (%)				
		Japan	*NIES 3*	*ASEAN*	*China*	*East Asia*
GDP	1980	10.0	1.3	1.8	2.9	16.0
	1990	13.3	2.1	1.5	1.7	18.6
	2000	14.8	3.0	1.8	3.4	23.0
Export	1980	6.6	2.5	3.5	0.9	13.4
	1990	8.6	4.8	3.8	1.7	18.8
	2000	6.7	5.0	5.8	6.0	23.4
Import	1980	6.3	2.7	3.1	1.1	13.2
	1990	6.2	4.2	4.1	1.3	16.2
	2000	5.0	4.1	4.8	4.1	18.9

Note: NIES 3 = South Korea + Taiwan + Hong Kong, ASEAN including Singapore.

Sources: GDP data from Kitahara and Nishizawa (2004, p. 280); trade data from Gaulier *et al.* (2004).

the intra-trade share of China-Japan-Korea is increasing faster than that of ASEAN 10. This is, again, due to the rapid growth of China in recent years (recall note 3 in Chapter 1).

Table 4.1 shows the recent trend in the relative changes of economic powers among East Asian countries in terms of GDP- and trade world shares. The top block of the table indicates that East Asia as a whole increased its world GDP share from 16.0 per cent in 1980 to 23.0 per cent in 2000, which is largely due to the significant increase in Japan's share from 10.0 per cent in 1980 to 14.8 per cent in 2000 as well as to that in NIES-3's share from 1.3 per cent to 3.0 per cent. China also increased its world GDP share from 2.9 per cent in 1980 to 3.4 per cent in 2004. (Although the world GDP share of China today is expected to be larger, the data are not available at hand.) In contrast, ASEAN's share remains the same over the same period. As a consequence, Japan's GDP share in East Asia was 62.5 per cent in 1980 whereas 64.3 per cent in 2000, implying that Japan's dominance of East Asia in terms of GDP share remained the same over the two decades.

In contrast with GDP share, trade shares provide a significantly different picture of East Asia. As the middle block of Table 4.1 shows, the world export share of East Asia grew in parallel with its world GDP share, from 13.4 per cent in 1980 to 23.4 per cent in 2004. However, its composition has changed dramatically over the same period. Although the world export share of Japan changed little from 1980 to 2002, the other three regions significantly increased their world export shares over the same period; in particular, China's world export share increased from 0.9 per cent in 1980 to 6.0 per cent in 2002. As a consequence, in 2002, Japan, NIES 3, ASEAN and China respectively occupy about the same share (i.e., about 6 per cent) of the world export share.

The bottom block in Table 4.1 provides roughly the same picture of East Asia in terms of world import shares as in terms of world export shares. However, all four countries/regions of East Asia have significantly smaller import shares than export shares. This means that East Asia as a whole has built up an export-platform to the rest of the world over the past quarter-century.

To see more precisely the export–import relationship within East Asia as well as with the rest of the world today, Table 4.2 presents the structure of world trade in 2004, with the focus on East Asia. The upper table represents the export structure, whereas the bottom table the import structure. We can see from Table 4.2 that while the world trade shares of EU25 (export share 40.0 per cent, import share 39.4 per cent) are the highest, the world trade share of East Asia (export share 26.4 per cent, import share 22.1 per cent) are much higher than those of NAFTA (export share 14.4 per cent, import share 20.7 per cent). It also shows that the US has the largest trade imbalance (6.8 per cent import surplus), while East Asia as a whole has the export surplus of 4.3 per cent.

Focusing on the countries/regions in East Asia, we can see from Table 4.2 that, in 2004, China exceeded Japan both in world export share and import share (export share: Japan 6.2 per cent vs. China 6.8 per cent, import share: Japan 4.6 per cent vs. China 5.8 per cent). In fact, in terms of world export share, China exceeded Japan for the first time in 2004, becoming the third largest exporter in the world after Germany and the US. In 2004, China was also the third largest importer in the world, after the US and Germany. We can also see from Table 4.2 that, for Japan in 2004, China is the second largest export-partner (13.3 per cent Japanese export share) after the US (22.7 per cent share), while China is the top import-partner for Japan (18.3 per cent Japanese import-share) ahead of the US (13.1 per cent share) or EU 25 (12.9 per cent share).

Although recently China attracts the most attention in the world trade area, we must notice that, in Asia today, each of Japan, NIES 3 (South Korea, Taiwan and Hong Kong), ASEAN 5 and China has

Table 4.2 The world trade structure in 2004

Regional composition of export

Export	World Share	East Asia	Japan	NIES 3	ASEAN 5	China	NAFTA	US	EU 25	ROW	total
East Asia	26.4	49.2	7.7	19.0	9.2	13.3	21.6	19.5	15.4	13.8	100.0
Japan	6.2	46.4	N/A	21.1	12.3	13.1	25.0	22.7	15.8	12.8	100.0
NIES 3	7.5	54.5	6.9	12.2	5.5	29.9	19.1	17.0	13.5	12.9	100.0
ASEAN 5	5.9	54.8	11.6	20.8	14.4	8.0	16.4	15.2	14.0	14.8	100.0
China	6.8	41.2	12.2	22.8	6.1	N/A	25.7	23.1	18.2	14.9	100.0
NAFTA	14.4	16.8	4.8	5.1	3.8	3.2	55.2	31.5	15.0	13.0	100.0
US	9.0	24.2	6.7	7.6	5.7	4.3	36.6	N/A	21.2	18.0	100.0
EU 25	40.0	6.2	1.5	1.7	1.4	1.7	9.2	7.9	67.0	17.6	100.0

Regional composition of import

Import	East Asia	Japan	NIES 3	ASEAN 5	China	NAFTA	US	EU 25
World Share	22.1	4.6	6.8	4.9	5.8	20.7	15.8	39.4
East Asia	58.9	44.6	73.7	49.8	60.6	27.6	32.6	10.3
Japan	13.1	N/A	19.3	15.6	14.0	7.5	8.9	2.5
NIES 3	18.5	11.3	13.5	8.4	38.5	6.9	8.0	2.6
ASEAN 5	14.6	14.9	18.0	17.3	8.1	4.6	5.6	2.1
China	12.8	18.3	23.0	8.5	N/A	8.5	10.0	3.2
NAFTA	11.0	15.1	10.7	11.1	7.9	38.4	28.6	5.5
US	9.8	13.1	10.0	10.4	6.6	15.9	N/A	4.8
EU 25	11.2	12.9	9.8	11.3	11.5	17.8	20.1	68.1
ROW	18.9	27.4	5.8	27.8	20.0	16.2	18.7	16.1
Total	100.0	100.0	100.0	100.0	100.0	100.0	100.0	100.0

Note: NIES 3 = South Korea + Taiwan + Hong Kong, ASEAN 5 = Malaysia + Thailand + Philippines + Indonesia + Singapore.

roughly the same size of world share both in export and in import. Thus, in terms of world trade, we can say that today's East Asia is a multi-cored economy, consisting of Japan, NIES 3, ASEAN 5 and China with each having roughly the same power in world trade. Notice also from Table 4.2 that, in 2004, 19.5 per cent of East Asia's export is to the US, whereas only 11.2 per cent of East Asia's import is from the US, resulted in a huge trade imbalance between the two regions/countries. In particular, 23.1 per cent of China's export is to the US, whereas only 6.6 per cent of China's import is from the US. This suggests that

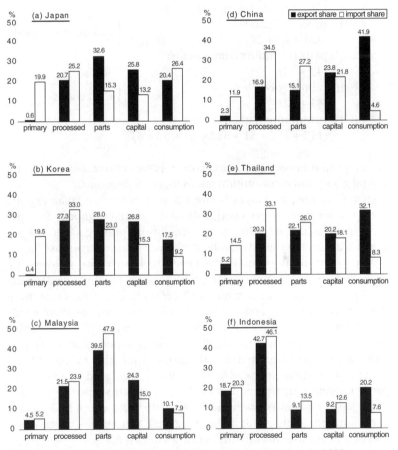

Figure 4.2 Trade structure of individual countries in East Asia in 2003

Note: Based on UNU-Broad Economic Categories.
Source: Data based on Table 2–3–1 in *White Paper on International Trade 2005*, METI, Japan.

recently China is used as the main export-platform of East Asia to the US (as well as to the EU).

To see the last point more precisely, let us examine the trade structure of East Asian countries more closely. Figure 4.2, which is based on the data from the *White Paper on International Economy and Trade 2005* by Japanese METI, shows the trade structure of representative countries in East Asia in 2003. In this figure, traded goods are classified into five categories based on production stages:

(i)   primary goods:
        (BEC code 111 + 21 + 31)
(ii-a) processed goods   ⎫
        (121 + 22 + 32)   ⎬ intermediate goods
(ii-b) parts (including components) ⎭
        (42 + 53)
(iii-a) capital goods   ⎫
        (41 + 521)   ⎬ final goods
(iii-b) consumption goods   ⎭
        (112 + 122 + 51 + 522 + 61 + 62 + 63)

We may call processed goods and parts together *intermediate goods*, and capital goods and consumption goods together *final goods*.

First, from the panel (a) in Figure 4.2, we can see that Japan exports parts the most (32.6 per cent), followed by capital goods (25.8 per cent), processed goods (20.7 per cent), consumption goods (20.4 per cent), with primary goods the least (0.6 per cent). In contrast, Japan imports consumption goods the most (26.4 per cent), followed by processed goods (25.2 per cent), primary goods (19.9 per cent), parts (15.3 per cent) and capital goods (13.2 per cent). This means that using the imported primary goods, Japan first produces intermediate goods (processed goods and parts), which are partly exported. A significant portion of the exported intermediate goods is imported back to Japan either as final goods or intermediate goods with higher values. Finally, using intermediate goods, which are partly produced in Japan and partly imported, Japan produces final goods, which are partly exported. Thus, Japan represents a typical country with *improvement trade*, where a lot of intermediate goods are moving back and forth between Japan and other countries (mostly the countries in East Asia).

In comparison of panels (a) and (b) in Table 4.2, we can see that Korea has a similar trade structure with Japan except that, in comparison to Japan, Korea's trade shares in processed goods are higher, whereas lower in consumption goods. Although Taiwan is missing in Figure 4.2, her trade structure is very similar to that of Korea.

Panel (c) reveals that, by far, Malaysia's largest exports and imports are of parts comparing panel (c) with the rest of panels, we can also see that both the export share (39.5 per cent) and import share (47.9 per cent) of parts in Malaysia's trade are the highest among the six countries. We can also see that both the export share (21.5 per cent) and import share (23.9 per cent) of processed goods in Malaysia are also very high. Thus, Malaysia imports a lot of intermediate goods, and then exports them again after adding more values. Although Singapore and Philippines are missing in Figure 4.2, they have a similar trade structure with Malaysia, where parts have the highest share in both export and import (35.2 per cent export share, 43.2 per cent import share for Singapore; 55.6 per cent export share, 48.8 per cent import share for Philippines).

We can see from panels (d) and (e) that China and Thailand have very similar trade structures. In both countries, processed goods occupy the highest import share (34.5 per cent for China, 33.1 per cent for Thailand), parts the next highest import share (27.2 per cent for China, 26.0 per cent for Thailand). Combining processed goods and parts together, intermediate goods have the important 61.7 per cent share for China, and 59.1 per cent for Thailand. In contrast, on the export side, consumption goods occupy the highest share in both countries (41.9 per cent for China, 32.1 per cent for Thailand), while capital goods the second highest share for China (23.8 per cent). Combining consumption goods and capital goods together, final goods have a 65.7 per cent of export share for China, and 52.3 per cent for Thailand. We can also see that both processed goods and parts have significant export shares for both countries. Thus, we can conclude that China and Thailand import mainly intermediate goods, and transform them into final goods, which in turn become the major export items for both countries; in addition, a significant portion of imported intermediate goods are reexported after adding more values.

Finally, panel (f) reveals that processed goods occupy nearly a half of both export and import for Indonesia. Furthermore, among the six countries in Figure 4.2, both export- and import shares of primary goods are the highest for Indonesia. Thus, the trade activity of Indonesia is focused mainly on the import and export of primary goods and processed goods.

Figure 4.2 represents the aggregate trade structure of each country with the rest of the world, not revealing individual trade partners.

However, given that the intra-trade share of East Asia is 52.4 per cent in 2003 (recall Figure 4.1), we can consider that, on average, more than a half of the imports and exports of each country in Figure 4.2 is with other countries in East Asia. Thus, we can conclude from Figure 4.2 that the East Asian countries have together developed a highly integrated production network system, in which Japan, NIES and ASEAN countries have complementary trade structures as a whole, while a lot of intermediate goods are moving back and forth within East Asia before yielding final goods.

Combining the information from Table 4.2 and Figure 4.2, we can develop Figure 4.3 which represents a rough picture of the trade pattern in the Asia-Pacific region with the focus on East Asia and the US. As noted previously, Japan, Asian NIES, China and ASEAN together have developed a highly integrated production system, in which intermediate goods are moving back and forth, while the final goods assembled in China and ASEAN (as well as in Japan and NIES) are exported to the US (as well as to the rest of the world.)[1] In particular, China became the largest export-platform of East Asia, resulting in the largest bilateral-trade imbalance between China and the US today.

Here, it must be pointed out that although China and ASEAN play the role of the main export platform of East Asia to the rest of the world today, large shares of their trade activity are conducted by the affiliates of multinational firms (MNFs) there. For example, in 2004, 57 per cent of both exports and imports of China were conducted by

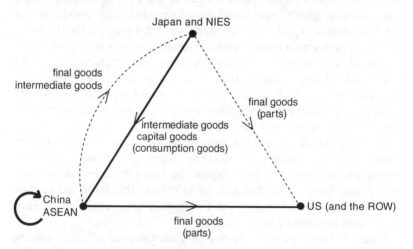

Figure 4.3   The triangular trade pattern in Asia-Pacific

the MNFs (Gaulier *et al.* 2004). Thus, we can conclude that over the past quarter-country, East Asia as a whole has developed a highly integrated production network system in which MNFs play a major role. In the next section, we examine how such a production system has been developed in East Asia.

Evolution of regional economies in East Asia: from the 'flying geese' to a multi-cored economy

In the proceeding section, we have seen that Japan, Asian NIES, China and ASEAN together have developed a highly integrated production network system in which intermediate goods are moving back and forth, while MNFs play a major role. Unlike the EU and NAFTA, East Asia has developed such a highly integrated production system mainly through market mechanisms, with little support from region-wide political institutions. In this section, we aim to understand from the standpoint of spatial economics how such a highly interdependent production system has been developed in East Asia over the past several decades. First we review the so called 'flying geese process' of economic development in East Asia from the 1970s to the early 1990s, and show that linkage-based agglomeration economies have been at work in the process of economic development in East Asia. In order to supplement the macro analyses of industrial location in the previous section we then focus on the nine largest Japanese electronics MNFs and study the transformation of their global production system from the 1970s to the 1990s. Finally, using more recent data, we show that recently East Asia as a whole is evolving towards a multi-cored economy.

Flying geese process of economic development in East Asia: Until the early 1990s

Although recently the spatial system of East Asian economy seems to be developing towards a multi-cored economy, the present spatial system has evolved through the process of the so called 'flying geese pattern' of international economic development started in the early 1960s. Figure 4.4 depicts this process of East Asia's economic development until the early 1990s, in which Japan played the role of the core economy or the 'lead goose'.

Although there seems to exist no clear definition of the flying geese pattern of economic development, here we loosely interpret it as follows.[2] A group of countries located in geographical proximity (in the

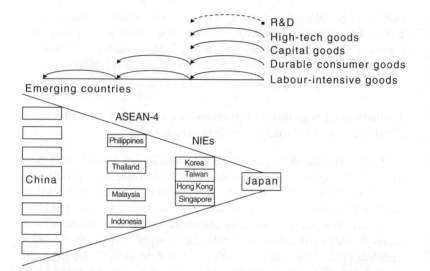

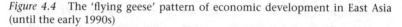

Figure 4.4 The 'flying geese' pattern of economic development in East Asia (until the early 1990s)

present case, East Asia) achieves a rapid economic growth, mainly through the market mechanism, by deepening the international division of labour in industrial production such that the most developed country (Japan), or the 'lead goose', becomes more and more specialized in technologically advanced industries by successively shedding industries in which she no longer holds a comparative advantage; these industries, in turn, locate in the nearby, less developed countries (Asian NIEs), or the 'following geese': in turn, over time, these developing countries upgrade their own industrial structures by themselves shedding outdated industries to the neighbouring, less developed countries (ASEAN and China), and so on.

Below, we provide empirical data that suggest that *linkage-based agglomeration economies* (explained in Chapter 1) have been playing a central role in such a process of economic development in East Asia.

We focus on Japan, and nine other countries in Asia (Asia-9): NIES 4 (Republic of Korea, Taiwan, Hong Kong and Singapore), ASEAN 4 (Philippines, Thailand, Malaysia and Indonesia), and China. We call Japan and Asia-9 countries together East Asia, of which the total population in 2000 was approximately 1.6 billion. Given that the distance between Tokyo and Bangkok is about the same as that between New York and San Francisco, East Asia has roughly the same geographical extent as that of the US.

Table 4.3   Concentration of economic activity within Japan and East Asia in 1990

	Japan share in East Asia	J-Core share within Japan	J-Core share in East Asia
Area (%)	3.5	5.2	0.18
Population	7.9	33	2.5
GDP	72	40	29
M-GDP	67	44	29

Sources: National Economic Statistics (Japanese EPA) and *Key Indicators of Developing Asian Pacific Countries* (Asian Development Bank).

The second column of Table 4.3 shows the extent of Japan's economic dominance in this region. That is, in 1990, Japan, having only a 3.5 per cent of the area and 7.9 per cent of the population of East Asia, accounted for the 72 per cent of the GDP, and 67 per cent of the manufacturing GDP. The third column, in turn, shows the extent of the dominance of the Japanese economy itself by its core region (J-Core). Here the J-Core represents the four prefectures (Tokyo, Kanagawa, Osaka and Hyogo) that contain the core parts of the three major metropolitan areas of Japan. As shown in the table, the J-Core with just a 5.2 per cent share of the area accounted for 33 per cent of the population, 40 per cent of GDP and 44 per cent of M-GDP (manufacturing GDP) of Japan in 1990. This leads to the fourth column, indicating that for the entire East Asia, the J-Core with a mere 0.18 per cent of total area accounted for 29 per cent of both GDP and M-GDP.

Given that (financial) capital became rather freely movable internationally by the early 1980s and that both labour and capital are almost perfectly mobile within Japan, these astonishing concentrations of economic activity in both Japan and the J-Core would be hard to explain without taking account of some kind of agglomeration economies.

To investigate the nature of such agglomeration economies, here we focus on manufacturing, and present in Figure 4.5 the regional structure of manufacturing industries in Japan and East Asia in 1985. The entire manufacturing is divided into 17 industries as shown at the bottom of the figure. The horizontal axis in the figure represents for each industry the GDP share of the J-Core region within Japan. The vertical axis for black dots shows for each industry the GDP share of Japan within East Asia; the vertical axis for white circles shows (for each industry) the GDP share of the ASEAN 4 plus China within East Asia.

We can see an apparent positive-correlation between the two indices for Japan, indicating that the more highly Japanese industries concentrate in the J-Core, the more strongly they dominate in East Asia. In contrast, the set of white circles for the ASEAN 4 plus China looks almost the mirror image of the set of black dots for Japan, implying that these countries are stronger in those industries that are less agglomerated in the J-Core.[3]

In particular, two groups of industries in the figure present interesting and contrasting cases for Japan. One is the machinery-metal group, consisting of industries 2, 3, 4, 5, 6 and 7, which locate together in the upper-middle (next to industry 1) of the figure. The position of this group of Japanese industries in the figure suggests another strong case of linkage-based agglomeration economies at work. In fact, Michael Porter (1990) discusses extensively how such linkage-based agglomeration economies have been realized by this group of industries in Japan.

The contrasting case is presented by the textile-apparel group (industries 11 and 12). Until the late 1950s, this textile-apparel group constituted a major part of manufacturing activity in both Japan and J-Core. In 1955, for example, this group accounted for 15 per cent of the total manufacturing GDP in Japan, of which 45 per cent was concentrated in the J-Core. As shown in the figure, however, in 1985 Japan was among the weakest in these industries (within East Asia), and they are among the least agglomerated in the J-Core.

Although Figure 4.5 is about 1985, let us also consider 1990 and 1993, and examine statistically how the relationship changed over time. To do so, let

$$X = \frac{GDP_{J\text{-}Core}}{GDP_J}, \quad Y = \frac{GDP_J}{GDP_{A9} + GDP_J}$$

X represents the measure on the horizontal axis in Figure 4.5, and Y the measure on the vertical axis for Japan (i.e. for black dots). Figure 4.5 indicates that X and Y exhibit a concave relationship. Hence, instead of a direct linear-regression of X and Y, let us introduce an intermediate variable

$$Z = \frac{GDP_J}{GDP_{A9}}$$

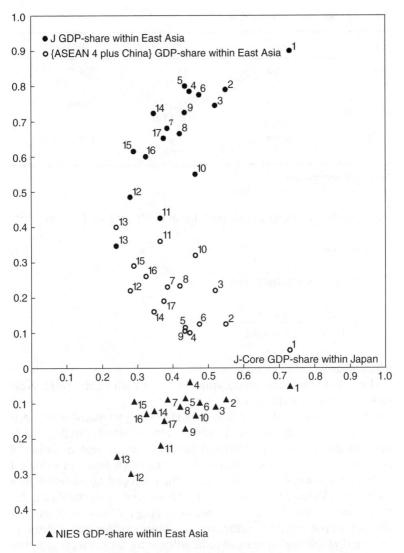

1. Publishing and printing, 2. Transport equipment, 3. Machinery (non-electrical),4. Electrical machinery, 5. Precision instruments, 6. Fabricated metal products, 7. Basic metal, 8. Chemical and chemical products, 9. Plastic products, 10. Rubber products, 11. Textile, 12. Wearing apparel, 13. Petroleum and coal products, 14. Paper and paper products, 15. Non-metallic mineral products 16. Food, beverage and Tobacco, 17. others.

Figure 4.5 Regional structure of manufacturing industries in Japan and East Asia in 1985

Sources: *Census of Manufactures* (Japan) and *Industrial Statistics Yearbook* (United Nations).

Table 4.4   Regression of equation 4.2

year	a	b	R^2
1985	−3.24	13.9** (t = 7.87)	0.885
1990	−2.17	12.1** (t = 7.79)	0.896
1993	−2.09	11.0** (t = 8.87)	0.917

Note: ** significant at 1%.

representing the ratio of Japanese GDP over A9 GDP, and assume that

$$Z = a + bX \qquad (4.1)$$

Then, it holds identically that

$$Y = \frac{Z}{1+Z} = \frac{a+bX}{1+a+bX}$$

which proves concavity in X.

The linear regression of equation (4.1) for each of the three years yields the results in Table 4.4.

We can see from Table 4.4 that there is a strong relationship between the degree of the dominance of each Japanese industry in Asia (measured by its GDP share in Asia) and the degree of the agglomeration of that industry in the J-Core. Furthermore, the coefficient b in Table 4.4 in 1985, for example, indicates that if the degree of agglomeration of an industry in the J-Core increases by 10 per cent, then the Z-ratio for that industry will become 139 per cent larger. However, Table 4.4 shows that the value of coefficient b becomes smaller with time, suggesting that the agglomeration economies of the J-Core relative to the rest of Japan and East Asia are weakening over time.[4]

Globalization of Japanese multinational firms from the mid 1970s to the early 1990s

In Chapter 1, using the theory of spatial economics, we examined the general effects of decreasing transport costs on the spatial distribution of economic activities. In particular, the theory of spatial economics indicates that large agglomerations of economic activities can emerge only when transport costs of products become sufficiently low. This explains the dominant agglomeration of major economic activities in Japan during the process of the 'flying geese' pattern of economic development in East Asia, as we have seen in the previous section. The theory of spatial economics also indicates that, with a further reduction of transport costs, many industries or labour intensive phases of production activities gradually shift from the core region (or the core country) to nearby peripheral regions, then to further peripheral regions. This partly explains why the agglomeration economies of the J-Core relative to the rest of Japan and East Asia were weakening through the 1980s and the 1990s, as we have seen in the last part of the previous section. In Chapter 1, we have also learned from the theory of spatial economics that the development of transport and information technologies tend to make major metropolises and advanced regions more dominant in knowledge-intensive activities. Furthermore, as explained in Chapter 1, the theory of spatial economics indicates that the sufficient advancement of transport and information technologies will lead to the rapid growth of multinational firms (MNFs), resulting in a major reorganization of the global production system and division of labour.

In this section, using micro data about Japanese MNFs, we aim to demonstrate that such complex effects of decreasing transport- and communications costs (which have been predicted by the theory of spatial economics) have actually happened through the process of the 'flying geese' pattern of economic development in East Asia. For this purpose, we focus here on the nine largest electronics firms in Japan, and study the transformation of their global production system over the period of 1975 to 1994. The firms considered are Hitachi, Matsushita Electric, Toshiba, NEC, Mitsubishi Electric, Fujitsu, Sony, Sanyo Electric and Sharp, total sales of which in 1990 were almost 200 billion dollars. The electronics industry has been the largest and most rapidly growing among all manufacturing industries in Japan since the mid 1970s, and has been dominated by the nine MNFs above.[5]

In Figures 4.6 and 4.7 respectively we present the changes in the global distribution of the production plants and R&D facilities of these nine firms between 1975 and 1994.

As can be seen from Figure 4.6, over the 19-year period from 1975 to 1994, the number of worldwide manufacturing plants owned by the nine Japanese firms increased more than twice from 285 to 689. In particular, while the number of domestic plants increased about 70 per cent (from 211 to 354), that of overseas plants jumped 4.5 times (from

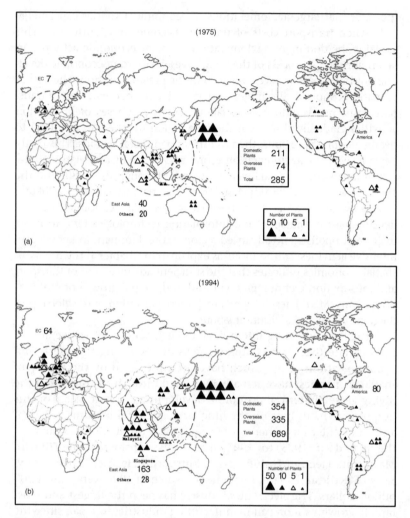

Figure 4.6   Location of the production plants of nine Japanese electronics firms in 1975 and 1994

Source: Fujita and Ishii (1999).

74 to 335). As a consequence, in 1994 the nine firms had roughly the same number of plants in Japan and overseas. Their overseas plants are mostly concentrated in East Asia, North America and the EU. The number of plants in East Asia increased greatly from 40 to 163, most of which have been serving as exporting platforms to the global markets

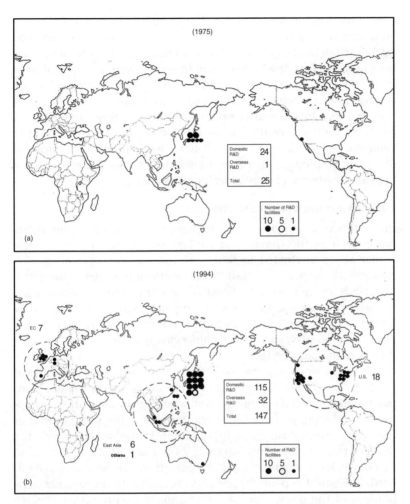

Figure 4.7   Location of R&D facilities of nine Japanese electronics firms in 1975 and 1994

Source: Fujita and Ishii (1999).

while taking advantage of low wages in the region. The number of plants in North America and the EU also increased greatly from 7 to 80 and from 7 to 64 respectively, to serve the big markets in these countries.

Next, Figure 4.7 indicates that over the same 19-year period, the nine firms greatly expanded their R&D capacity in Japan (from 24 to 115 laboratories) and in the USA (from 1 to 18, mostly located in California State and the Northeast Coast). Several R&D laboratories were also established in the EU. The number of overseas R&D laboratories (of the nine firms) in East Asia is very small in comparison with that of their manufacturing plants, which indicates the spatial division of labour among global regions being developed by the firms.

In this way, by the mid 1990s, each of the nine firms developed an advanced global network for the integrated operation of its entire value-chain including the management, R&D, production, procurement, distribution, sales operations worldwide, which is based on the modern transport and communications technologies.

Towards a multi-cored East Asia

In the proceeding two sections, we have examined the 'flying geese' process of industrial development in East Asia, in which Japan (in particular MNFs originated in Japan) played the role of 'lead goose'. However, this process of industrial development has been so successful that, since the mid 1990s, East Asia's economy as a whole started being transferred from the previous mono-polar system (dominated by Japan) to a multi-cored system. In this section, again, we focus on the electronics industry, and examine more closely its development in East Asia since the early 1990s.

In the electronics industry, here we focus on two major categories of products, i.e., information processors (including PCs, main-frame computers and peripheral equipment) and wireless communications equipments (including portable telephones). In 2002, the world output of the electronics industry was 1,047 billion US dollars, in which the share of information processors was 28 per cent ($302 billion), and that of wireless communications equipments was 16 per cent ($168 billion). In Figure 4.8, panel (a) presents the change in the regional composition of the production of information processors from 1990 to 2002, and panel (b) that of wireless communications equipment.

Panel (a) indicates that East Asia-11 (i.e., East Asia excluding Japan) has achieved a phenomenal growth in the production of information processors since 1990, resulting in 43 per cent of world share in 2002, exceeding the combined share of NAFTA (25 per cent) and the EU 15 (15 per cent). In contrast, although Japan had the highest share (29.5 per cent) in 1990, her share decreased gradually to 13 per cent in 2002, which is partly due to the expansion of overseas production by Japanese MNFs. Among the East Asia-11, the growth of China (including Hong Kong) has been most phenomenal, with her share (17.5 per cent)

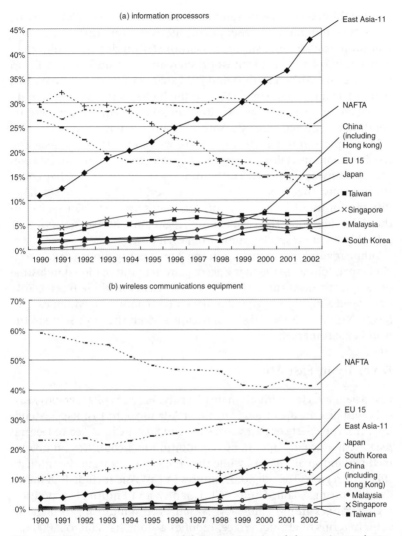

Figure 4.8 Regional composition of the two categories of electronics products

Note: East Asia-11 represents China, Hong Kong, India, Indonesia, Malaysia, Singapore, South Korea, Taiwan, Thailand and Vietnam.
Source: Imai and Kawakami (2005).

exceeding Japanese share for the first time in 2002. In East Asia in 2002, after China and Japan, Taiwan has the next highest share, followed by Singapore, Malaysia and South Korea.

Panel (b) in Figure 4.8 presents a significantly different picture of the wireless-communications-equipments industry (from that of the information-processors industry in panel (a)). This industry is still dominated by NAFTA (41 per cent world share in 2002), and then by EU 15 (23 per cent). Although the combined share of East Asia-11 overtook that of Japan in 2000, Japan still had the highest share among all individual countries in East Asia in 2002. In 2002, Japan was followed by South Korea, China, Malaysia, Singapore and then by Taiwan.

In comparison of panels (a) and (b), we can see that East Asia as a whole is more specialized in information processors than wireless communications equipments. Furthermore, among all East Asian countries/regions, their relative rankings in world share are considerably different in the two categories of electronics products. Thus, even in the electronics industry, each country/region in East Asia shows a considerably different specialization from each other.

Summarizing the discussions in the 2 previous sections, we can conclude that, following the flying geese pattern of international industrial development until the early 1990s, East Asia as a whole has recently developed a highly integrated multi-cored economy in which each of Japan, NIES 3, ASEAN and China occupies about the same share of the world export market.

Diversity in East Asia

East Asia is a region with ultimate diversity. In terms of geography, East Asia contains the area from North East Asia to South East Asia, extending form the coasts of East China Sea and South China Sea to Central Asia, with a dozen large islands in addition to a countless number of medium and small islands, while the climate ranges from the tropic to subarctic region. The religions/cultures in East Asia include Buddhism, Confucianism, Islam, Hindu, Christianity and Shinto. The political regime ranges from democracy, socialism, communism, to dictatorship. In terms of ethnicity/race, Indonesia alone has 200 to 2,000 different races (depending on how one counts). Languages includes Chinese with several dialects, Malayan, Indonesian, Korean, Japanese and English. Most importantly here, there is a huge disparity in income among countries and regions reflecting the different level of productivity.

Figure 4.9 shows the GDP per capita by country (in terms of US$) in East Asia in 2002. The GDP per capita in Japan is about 100 times higher than that in Cambodia, and about 30 times higher than that in China, for example. Such big disparities in GDP per capita reflect the

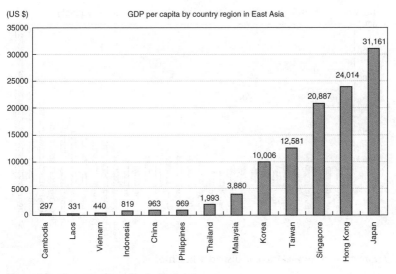

Figure 4.9   Income disparity in East Asia

Source: Based on data from *World Development Indicators 2004*, World Bank.

productivity difference (measured in US$) among countries, which in turn reflects partly the difference in the level of human capital development, and partly the difference in the level of agglomeration economies enjoyed in each country today. The ordering of countries in Figure 4.9 in terms of GDP per capita roughly reflects the historical order of industrial development implied by the flying geese pattern of economic development depicted in Figure 4.4. This illustrates that today's spatial structure of an economy is highly dependent on the historical process of economy development.

In contrast, among EU-15 countries in 2001, the GDP per capita in Luxembourg (the highest) is about 3 times of that in Greece (the lowest). Even among EU-25 countries in 2001, the GDP per capita in Luxembourg is about 9 times of that in Romania (the lowest). Thus, the income disparity in East Asia is far greater than that in Europe.

Not only among countries but also within each country of East Asia, there is a large disparity in income. Figure 4.10 represents the GDP per capita in each municipality and province in China in 2003. The GDP per capita in Shanghai is about 13 times higher than that in Guizhou Province. For another example, Figure 4.11 shows the GDP per capita in Indonesia in 2000. The GDP per capita in DKJ Jakarta is 13 times higher than that in Nusa Tenggara Timur. Comparing Figures 4.10

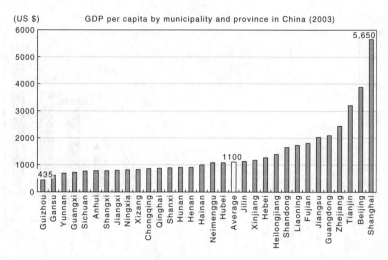

(US $)   GDP per capita by municipality and province in China (2003)

Figure 4.10   Regional income disparity in China

Source: Chinese Annual Statistics 2004.

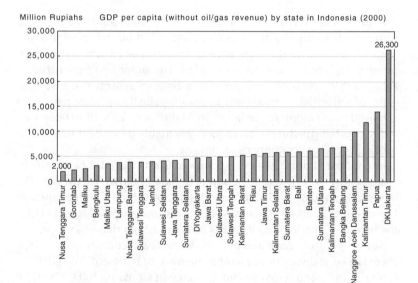

Million Rupiahs   GDP per capita (without oil/gas revenue) by state in Indonesia (2000)

Figure 4.11   Regional income disparity in Indonesia

Source: Statistik Indonesia (2004).

and 4.11 shows that China and Indonesia have a similar structure of regional income disparity.

Such a huge diversity in East Asia in many dimensions provides both big challenges and big opportunities in further integration of East Asia, as discussed in the next section.

Further promotion of regional integration in East Asia

Until the mid 1990s, the regional economic integration of East Asia was promoted, in a de facto manner, mainly through trade and investment under the framework of the WTO. However, starting with the agreement on the formation of ASEAN Free Trade Area (AFTA) in 1992, the efforts for creating bilateral FTAs involving East Asian countries increased rapidly. Furthermore, in addition to bilateral FTAs, the development of ideas on an Asian-wide cooperative framework for further promotion of regional integration in East Asia became increasingly serious. Recently, both policy markers and businessmen started talking about the possibility of creating an 'Asian Community'. Such a shift in international policies in East Asia was caused by several factors.

First, given the slow progress in the further promotion of free trade under the WTO framework, East Asian countries also realized the need for the development of bilateral FTAs while complementing the WTO framework. Second, the creation of the EU, NAFTA and MERCOSUR made East Asia relatively disadvantageous in international trade and investment. Third, in order to anchor and to further promote the economic integration that has been achieved mainly through the market mechanism, the development of an Asianwide institutional framework for mutual cooperation has become indispensable. In particular, after the financial crisis in Asia in 1997, the establishment of an Asianwide institutional framework for financial stability became urgent. Fourth, in addition to the problem of financial stability in Asia, many new Asianwide problems have appeared recently. These problems include issues on security, environment, energy, SARS and bird-influenza, which can be solved successfully only through Asianwide cooperative frameworks. Finally, it is increasingly realized that Asianwide cooperative schemes are indispensable for promoting the economic development and political stability of less-developed countries and regions in East Asia.

In Part II of the symposium, considering these issues, three panelists from China, Korea and Thailand together with Paul Krugman and

Anthony Venables discuss the prospects and tasks of regional integration in East Asia.

Notes

1. Although it is obvious that the US and the ROW also export their products to East Asia, this aspect is omitted in Figure 4.3 in order to emphasize that East Asia as a whole has developed an integrated export-platform to the world.
2. As is well-known, the term 'flying geese' originates in the 'flying geese theory' of economic development proposed by Akamatsu (1962). Here, our interpretation essentially follows that of Hatch and Yamamura (1996, p. 27). The flying geese theory is closely related to the 'product cycle theory' introduced by Vernon (1966). The former observes the same phenomena from the view point of a developing country, while the latter from the view point of a developed country.
3. Given that Asian NIES 4 are relatively specialized in industries 9, 10, 11, 12 and 13, no clear correlation exists between the two indices for this group of countries. Notice also that industry 10 is rather exceptional in Figure 4.5 because this industry includes both synthetic rubber and crude rubber, the former (the latter) is relatively strong in Japan (in ASEAN).
4. For a similar study using the data in more recent years, see Chapter 1 in *White Paper on International Economy and Trade* 2005, METI, Japan.
5. Our discussion below includes the activities of the worldwide subsidiaries of these nine firms. Furthermore, throughout this section, the term 'electronics' should be understood broadly to include both electric and electronic products.

References

Akamatsu, K. (1962) 'A historical pattern of economic *growth in developing countries*', *Developing Economies*, 1(Mar.–Aug.), 3–25.

Fujita, M. and R. Ishii (1999) 'Global location behavior and organizational dynamics of Japanese electronics firms and their impact on regional economies', in A. D. Chandler, P. Hagström and Ö. Sölvell (eds), *The Dynamic Firm*, Oxford: Oxford University Press, 343–83.

Gaulier, G., F. Lemoine and D. Ünal-Kesenci (2004) 'China's integration in Asian production networks and its implications', Centre d'études Prospectives et d'information internationales (mimeo).

Hatch, W. and K. Yamamura (1996) *Asia in Japan's Embrace: Building a Regional Production Alliance*, Cambridge: Cambridge University Press.

Imai, K. and M. Kawakami (2005) *Development Process of Information Machinery Industry in East Asia*, Chiba, Japan: Institute of Developing Economies, JETRO (in Japanese).

Kitahara, A. and N. Nishizawa (2004) *Economic Theory of Asia*, Tokyo: Minerba Shobo (in Japanese).

Porter, M. E. (1990) *The Competitive Advantage of Nations*, New York: The Free Press.

Vernon, R. (1966) 'International investment and international trade in the product cycle', *Quarterly Journal of Economics*, 80, 190–207.

Part II

Prospects and Tasks of Regional Integration in East Asia

5
Regional Integration from a Chinese Perspective

Yu Yongding

Introduction

We know why nations trade with and invest in each other. We also know why trade liberalization is beneficial to all trading partners. However, it is still worthwhile to ask why we should promote regional economic integration in an age of globalization. To answer this question, we should also ask whether there is an underlined 'law of movement' consisting of the interactions of economic forces, which will more or less inevitably lead to regional economic integration in a given region; or whether regional economic integration is simply a result of conscientious efforts made by related countries. The theory of economic geography developed by Krugman, Fujita and Venables seems to have provided a general answer to the question. The key element of the answer is that distance matters. According to Krugman, the importance of distance, and the success of gravity models, explains the rapid growth of trade among East Asian economies, and particularly Asian trade with China. According to the theory of economic geography, if two economies grow fast, their mutual trade will grow very fast. And if they are relatively close geographically, their mutual trade will quickly become a major part of world trade, whether or not there are any special affinities or links (Krugman, 2004). However, economic geography alone does not explain why at certain period of time, certain specific countries will participate in economic integration in a specific form. The answer to East Asian economic cooperation and integration goes beyond economic geography. According to Sakakibara and Yamakawa (2004), integration processes in Europe and East Asia developed along different paths. In Europe, governments and their policies, including the early creation of regional institutions, drove the process

91

of the integration. In East Asia, the driving force behind integration has been the market, or more specifically, multinational corporations and their production networks.

While agreeing with Sakakibara and Yamakawa on the pivotal rule of market forces in driving integration in East Asia, I would also like to emphasize the importance of national government policies in shaping the progress of economic integration in the region. Without government initiatives, East Asian economic integration would fail to go this far. Equally true is the fact that because of a lack of political will, East Asian economic integration failed to go very far. When studying the issue of optimum currency areas, some studies found that the Eurozone is not an Optimum Currency Area (OCA) (Kiss 2000), but that East Asian countries can form a monetary union without incurring so much opportunity costs of losing monetary independence and policy autonomy (Trivisvavet, 2001). These seemingly-unexpected conclusions in fact are not surprising at all. As Frankel and Rose (1997) point out 'Trade patterns and income correlations are endogenous ... A country could fail the OCA criterion for membership today, and yet, if it goes ahead and joins anyway, as the result of joining, pass the OCA criterion in the future.' When we look at the process of regional economic integration in East Asia, the evidence to support the endogenous theory is abundant. Similar to the Eurozone, political decisions and institution building efforts have a significant role to play in fostering the market forces that drive East Asian regional economic integration.

The first section of the chapter discusses the breakdown of the traditional pattern of division of labour in the East Asian region and the emerging of regional production networks in the region. In the second section, China's place in the regional division of labour is discussed in terms of FDI and trade. The third section discusses China's policy towards regional economic integration, especially its efforts in establishing Free Trade Areas and financial cooperation in the region. The fourth section discusses obstacles to progress in regional economic integration from the perspective of international balances or imbalances. The last section is a short concluding one.

The changing pattern of economic relationship in East Asia

It was Akamatsu (1943) who first used the phrase 'wild geese pattern' of industrial development to describe the shape of import, production and export growth curves for a country. Kojima (1973) renamed the pattern the catching-up product cycle (CPC) after associating it with the product cycle model of Vernon (1964). The CPC model identifies five stages of development for a country: *introductory, import substitution, export, mature,* and *reverse import* in terms of production–demand ratio. Factors such as learning-by-doing, transfer of technology, FDI, accumulation of physical and human capital, changes in cost of production and so on contribute to the shift from one stage in the cycle of industrial development to the next in a country.

Changes in the trade structure go hand in hand with those of the industrial structure. According to Yamazawa (1990), three stages in Japan's pattern of trade can be identified. The first stage consists of the export of primary products and the import of light-industrial goods. The second consists of the export of light industrial goods and import of heavy industrial goods as well as raw materials. The export of heavy industrial goods and imports of raw materials characterize the third stage. The development gaps of economies in the East Asian region means that they are in different stages of the product cycle in their respective industries at a given period of time, thus giving rise to possibilities for forming a close regional network of trade and investment based on the vertical division of labour in the region. Products and capital flows in and out across borders in line with the flying geese pattern that in turn is consistent with Heckscher–Ohlin model as well as Vernon's product cycle theory.

The flying geese formation in the East Asian region was led by Japan. Starting with the manufacturing of simple labour-intensive goods for export, Japanese companies reinvested the profits to upgrade their capital stock and exported more sophisticated capital-intensive and technology-intensive goods. As a first-mover, initially, there was no problem for Japanese companies to export their products to the global and regional markets, under the circumstances of the time. Improvement in the terms of trade helped Japan to raise its income level. As a result of the rise in wages and living standards, Japan lost its comparative advantage in labour-intensive industries, which provided opportunities for later comers to fill the vacuum. Hong Kong, Singapore, South Korea and Chinese Taipei followed Japan. Then Malaysia, Thailand, the Philippines and Indonesia followed the newly industrializing economies (NIEs).

In the 1980s, a new pattern of regional division of labour began to take shape. As a result of the wave of liberalization of trade and investment that swept across the borders of the region, and especially, China's opening up, Japanese companies that were under tremendous competitive pressure, due to the appreciation of the yen since the 1985

Plaza Accord, were able to move production facilities to Asia to take the advantage of lower production costs. The technology revolution is one of the most important impetuses to the emergence of the new pattern of regional division of labour. The lowering of communication and transportation costs, the liberalization of trade and investment regimes that reduced transaction costs, the nature of new products (lighter and smaller for products with the same utilities) and change of technology (production process is more separable) lowered dramatically the 'cost of service links (SL) connecting production blocks (PB)', enabled corporations to fragment and internalize the production process (Ando and Kimura, 2003) and made distance a much less important factor in their 'location decision'. Clustering or agglomeration effect reduced the importance of comparative advantage in choosing production location by multinationals. It seems that both the rapid development of technological creativity and innovation that is global in nature and its *limitation*, have worked together to become a centrifugal force for regional economic integration.

The most important feature of the regional production networks is the so-called fragmentation of production process. According to Deardorff (1998), fragmentation refers to a production process that leads to the same final products but is split into many steps that can be undertaken in different locations. Each value chain or 'module', rather than the final product as a whole, becomes the focus in choosing production sites. As a result, trade of parts and components of the same products across borders become prevalent. Though the new pattern of regional division of labour fails to falsify the principle of comparative advantage, it has added new dimensions onto it. The changes in regional trade pattern provide support for the existence of the new regional production networks. Fukao *et al.* (2003) decompose bilateral trade into inter-industry trade (one-way trade), vertical intra-industry trade (VIIT) and horizontal intra-industry trade (HIIT). They show that Japanese and US FDI in East Asia is 'vertical' in the sense that manufacturing affiliates are established in order to take VIIT advantage of cheap labour, and the majority of output is exported to their home countries or other countries. Japan played the role of the provider of capital and technology to the NIEs and then the ASEAN four as well as an organizer of productions in the region. The major players in the FDI-VIIT and HIIT process are Japanese corporations in machinery industries including general machinery, electrical machinery, transport equipment and precision machinery. Japanese manufacturers not only export parts and components to the rest of East Asian economies for processing and assembly, but also set up production facilities to produce parts and components in the region and export them back to Japan. To a very large extent, the new pattern of regional production networks is shaped by Japanese FDI outflows in the region. The most visible changes in the trade pattern that supports the argument for the new regional production networks is the rapid increase in processing or assembly trades in the East Asian region. This is reflected in the explosive rise in trade of machinery goods, especially in trade of parts and components, after having separated the trade for parts and

Table 5.1   Dynamics of the Korea–China–Japan–ASEAN intra-trade intensity index

	Year	Korea	China	Japan	ASEAN
Korea	1980	–	0.08	2.39	1.97
	1985	–	0.06	2.23	1.56
	1991	–	0.78	2.61	2.02
	1996	–	2.84	1.88	2.03
	2001	–	3.22	1.98	1.92
China	1980	0.12	–	2.90	2.00
	1985	1.01	–	3.30	3.20
	1991	0.32	–	2.17	1.16
	1996	0.79	–	3.17	0.88
	2001	2.02	–	3.21	1.19
Japan	1980	3.59	3.71	–	3.05
	1985	2.47	3.18	–	1.98
	1991	2.79	1.52	–	2.41
	1996	2.57	1.88	–	2.63
	2001	2.86	1.98	–	2.59
ASEAN	1980	1.42	1.02	3.64	–
	1985	1.90	1.63	3.61	–
	1991	1.54	1.12	2.71	–
	1996	1.28	1.12	2.18	–
	2001	1.71	1.40	2.45	–

Notes: 1. The trade intensity index of country i is defined as $TII_{ij} = \dfrac{X_{ij} / X_i}{M_j / M_w}$ where X_{ij} is export from country i to j, X_i is total export of country i, M_j is total import of country j, M_w is world total import. TII_{ij} compares export from country i to j divided by total export of country i to the ratio of import of country j divided by total world import. If TII_{ij} is greater than 1 then country i and j are related more closely than others. The index was computed using IMF, *Direction of Trade Statistics Yearbook* (various issues).
2. ASEAN data represent Indonesia, Malaysia, Philippines and Thailand.

components from that of products in the machinery and transport sector (SITC7) and in the miscellaneous goods sector (SITC8) of manufacturing trade (Sakakibara and Yamakawa, 2004). According to Athukorala (2003), East Asia's share of world exports of parts and components increased from 34.4 per cent in 1992 to 39.5 per cent in 2000, while the region's share of world imports of parts and components remained unchanged over the same period (33.5 per cent and 33.1 per cent). More relevant to the concept of regional production networks, evidence, based on sectoral and corporation data or country-specific case studies, shows a significant increase in intra-regional trade (Table 5.1), especially in that of machinery goods (SITC7) and parts and components in machinery goods, although more systematic data are unavailable.

However, it is worth emphasizing that the new pattern of trade and investment has not entirely replaced the traditional pattern of inter-industrial trade and investment, and inter-regional trade and investment still holds an important place in the region. As a result, one-way trade, VIIT and HIIT coexist in the region. Furthermore, despite the fact that Japanese firms are playing a central role in shaping regional economic integration, owning to the active participation by American and European firms in the region, the process of regional economic integration is paralleled and interacted with that of global economic integration. The existing economic relationship in the East Asian region is far from pointing to an inevitability of regional economic integration.

China's role in regional economic integration

Since its opening up and reform, China has emerged as one of the most important factors in changing the economic relationship in the East Asian region. In the 1980s, China's trade pattern can be depicted roughly by the flying geese pattern. China imported capital goods in heavy industries and production lines in electronic industries, with an aim to substitute imports. At the same time, mainly via joined ventures with Hong Kong, Chinese enterprises started to enter international production and distribution networks.

FDI

Attracted by a huge army of cheap and skilled labour, increasingly more preferential policy, much-improved infrastructures, FDI inflows

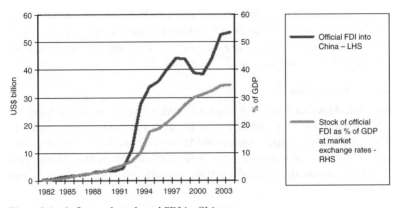

Figure 5.1   Inflows of stock and FDI in China

Source: Erskinomics.

into China have been increased steadily since the early 1990s. The bulk of FDI inflows is a result of fragmentation of production process, globally and regionally. The Chinese government's policy in favour of processing trade facilitated the inflows correspondingly. In 2003, FDI inflows into China was 56.14 billion US dollars, registering a 2.05 per cent increase over the previous year (Figure 5.1).

Sources of FDI

In the 1980s, the single most important source of FDI in China was Hong Kong (China). In the 1990s, FDI from Hong Kong, Taiwan (China), Singapore and other parts of East Asia, a region where there are large numbers of ethnic Chinese, still accounted for over 50 per cent of total FDI in China. However, the relative importance of these sources has declined since the later 1990s, especially after China's entry into the WTO, with the significant increase in FDI from the United States, the European Union and Japan. Over the past several years, except for a significant increase in Korea's FDI, the pattern of sources of China's FDI inflows has basically not changed.

Hong Kong

During the 1980s and early 1990s, Hong Kong was by far the largest source of FDI in China. Up to 1992, the share of FDI in China from Hong Kong was almost 70 per cent. Hong Kong contributed nearly half of the cumulated FDI in China during the past two decades. Currently, Hong Kong is still the most important source of FDI in China.

However, since the second half of the 1990s, major industrial countries' contribution to China's FDI inflows has increased significantly. In 2003, FDI inflows from Hong Kong were 17.7 billion, but their share in China's total FDI dropped to 34 per cent.

The United States

In 1992, America's FDI in China was US$500 million, accounting for only 4.6 per cent of China's total attraction of FDI in that year. In 2003, FDI inflows from the United States reached US$4.4 billion and accounted for 8 per cent of China's total attraction of FDI. The United States has been the second or third largest investor in China since 1998.

The European Union

In 1992, FDI from the EU accounted for only 2.2 per cent of China's total FDI. Its share in China's total FDI increased from 2.4 per cent in 1993 to 9.2 per cent in 1996. From 1997 on, FDI from the EU held stable at roughly US$4 billion a year. In 2003, EU direct investment in China increased to US$4.69 billion and accounted for 8.9 per cent of China's total FDI inflows.

Japan

In 1992, Japan's direct investment in China was US$710 million, second only to direct investment by Hong Kong and 1.4 times as high as direct investment by the United States. Japan's FDI in China peaked

Table 5.2   Japanese investment in China

Year	The value of investment ($US mil)	The share of Japan's FDI (%)
1993	1691	4.7
1994	2565	6.3
1995	4473	8.8
1996	2510	5.2
1997	1987	3.7
1998	1065	2.6
1999	751	1.1
2000	402	1.5*

Note: * shows the first half of 2000.

Source: Japan External Trade Organization White Paper on Foreign Direct Investment.

in 1997. Since then Japan's FDI in China has dropped dramatically, while other major investors have increased their investment in China. In 2003, FDI from Japan reached US$5.1 billion, which accounted for more than 9 per cent of China's total FDI inflows in that year. It should be pointed out that Japan's FDI in China is far from stable. In the middle of the 1990s, Japan's direct investment in China once dropped very significantly. The share of Japan's direct investment in China in Japan's overall overseas investment also diminished. Japan's direct investment in China amounted to US$ 4.47 billion in 1995 and accounted for 8.8 per cent of Japan's total overseas direct investment. It drastically reduced to US$ 751 million in 1999, which accounted only 1.1 per cent of Japan's total overseas direct investment (Table 5.2) (Chang, 2001). It was not until after 2000 did Japan's FDI in China recover strongly.

Other countries and regions

In addition to the above-mentioned economies, Taiwan (China), the Republic of Korea, and many other economies have become important sources of foreign direct investment in China. In order of the magnitude of their investment, these sources are Hong Kong, the United States, Japan, Taiwan, Korea, Germany, the United Kingdom, France, Australia, and Canada. Over the past several years, except for a significant increase in Korea's FDI, the pattern of sources of China's FDI inflows has basically not changed (Table 5.3)

Table 5.3   Sources of China's FDI inflows (%), 2001–2003

	2002	2003
ROW	25.53	25.84
Hong Kong	33.86	33.08
Taiwan	7.53	6.31
Singapore	4.43	3.85
South Korea	5.16	8.39
Japan	7.94	9.45
US	10.28	7.85
UK	1.70	1.39
Germany	1.76	1.60
France	1.09	1.13
Australia	0.72	1.11

Source: Ministry of Commerce, Government of China, 2003.

The factors contributing to China's success in attracting FDI

It can be seen that FDI from East Asia accounted for more than 53 per cent of the total inflows. Furthermore, relative to their economic sizes, the share of China's FDI inflows from East Asian economies is much higher than that from North America and Europe. This result is in line with the prediction based on the theory of economic geography.

However, distance cannot explain the specific dynamics of China's success in attracting FDI. There are many country-specific reasons. First, low-cost skilled labour is the single most attractive element for foreign companies to make goods in China. In China more than 20 million workers in urban areas enter the labour market, and there are many times more rural migrants who are moving around the county to search for jobs. Heavy competition among workers has kept wages very low. For example, in Guangdong province, one of the most important FDI hosting provinces in China, the wage levels are around $60 to $90 a month, and this figure has virtually not risen for nearly 10 years (Kuroda, 2000). China's advantage in the supply of white-collar workers is also very great. China has always emphasized the importance of higher education and vocational education. Illiteracy is relatively low countrywide, and technical and managerial workers are being trained in large numbers. More than 1,000 Chinese universities turn out over 900,000 graduates every year. The army of engineers is abundant in supply. Second, after spending two decades in building up its infrastructure, China has developed into a place for one-stop shopping. Companies can obtain everything in China, from raw materials to packaging and get their products to customers anywhere in the globe almost as conveniently as in a developed country. Third, China's preferential policy toward FDI is another important factor contributing to China's attractiveness as a recipient of FDI. These policies include income tax exemption or reduction, tariff exemption or reduction, value-added tax rebate and preferential loans. Fourth, the huge domestic market has become the most important attraction in recent years. After entry to the WTO, many multinationals have shifted their sights to China's domestic market, which has become more lucrative than one could possibly have imagined even a few years ago. Already China is the world's biggest cellular telephone market, and it is expected to surpass Japan as the second-biggest personal computer market. China buys more film than the Japanese and as many vehicles as the Germans. China even ranks very high in high-end luxury durable markets. For example, China is the third largest market for Bentley, the luxury-car maker.

FDI inflows have changed China's industrial landscape. The self-sufficient industrial system has long gone. China's manufacturing sector has become highly segmented. China is increasingly integrated into international production networks. As a result, processing trade dominates China's international trade. However, it seems that the FDI inflows failed to confine China in regional production networks. Rather, China together with East Asia is integrated into the global production networks. There seems to be no self-contained regional production networks in East Asia, which is reflected in the existence of the so-called trilateral imbalances among China, the rest of East Asia and the US.

Trade

Over the past two decades, China has made impressive headway in exports. The other East Asian economies are the most important trade partner of China. In the past ten years the shares of China's trade with the rest of East Asian economies accounted for 55 per cent to 60 per cent of its total trade. Despite the fact that the share of imports from the rest of Asia in China's total imports has been declining slightly, China's trade relationship with the rest of East Asia has been quite stable in terms of the shares of China's exports and imports to and from the rest of East Asia in its total exports and imports.

Naturally, China's export drive started with textile products and some other labour intensive products. In the 1990s, as a result of massive pushes of Japanese assembly lines in the 1980s, China witnessed excess capacity and improved competitiveness. Furthermore, the export of electronic and electric products has dominated China's exports of manufacturing goods. Up until the early 1990s, China's exports and imports seem to have followed the flying geese formation.

The most important category of exports by foreign funded enterprises is manufacturing goods, both in terms of the absolute value of exports and relative to domestic enterprises. In 2000, while the value of exports by foreign funded enterprises was US$194.4 billion, accounting for 48 per cent of China's total exports in the year, the value of manufacturing exports by foreign funded enterprises was US$ 99.1 billion, accounting for 82.99 per cent of foreign funded enterprises' total exports and 40 per cent of China's total exports in the year.

Because of the emergence of an international production network and China's policy in favour of processing trade, China's exports are dominated by processing trade. In 1980, China's total value of processing trade was US$1.66 billion. By 2001, the value was US$241.4 billion, a 145-fold increase. The share of processing trade in China's total trade increased from 4.4 per cent in 1980 to 47.4 per cent in 2001 (Development Research Centre of the State Council 2003, 6). In the 1990s, China's foreign trade expansion relied mainly on processing trade. Since the second half of the 1990s, processing trade has accounted for more than half of China's exports.

The close relationship between processing trade and FDI inflows is evident from China's trade structure. The fastest growth of exports came from electrical machinery, other transportation equipment, and instruments, which are sectors dominated by foreign funded enterprises. Correspondingly, imports of capital goods, semi-finished goods, and materials for processing exports grew very fast. For example, as a result of Japanese companies' shift of production – together with those from the United States and Taiwan – toward China, since the second half of the 1990s, China has emerged as the largest supplier of Japanese electronic components in Asia.

The production network established by leading Taiwan electronic firms across the Taiwan straits is another good example. Chinese Taipei has been referred to as the world's PC factory since it produces 70 per cent of the motherboards and 50 per cent of the notebook PCs sold around the world. Taiwan's information technology equipment makers have moved production of the most price-sensitive products, particularly desktop computers to Mainland China. The overseas production as a percentage of total output by Taiwanese firms has been increasing steadily from just above 25 per cent in 1995 to more than 50 per cent in 2000. The lion's share of the increase in overseas production went to

Table 5.4   IT products manufactured in mainland China as percentage of total output by Taiwanese firms: as of 2000

Product	Percentage manufactured in mainland China
Power outlets	90
Scanners	85
CD-ROMs	72
Cabinets	71
Monitors	56
Motherboards	46
Desktop PCs	45
Digital cameras	42
Notebooks	0

Note: Taiwan lifted the ban on producing notebook PCs in mainland China in 2001.

Sources: *The Nikkei Business Daily*; *The Nikkei Weekly*, 2001 July 23, p. 18.

Mainland China. Taiwanese firms made 45 per cent of the desktop PCs, 40 per cent of the motherboards and 85 per cent of the scanners in China in 2000 (Table 5.4) (*Nikkei Weekly*, 2001)

The impact of China's export drive on its neighbours is multi-dimensional. In labour-intensive products, Chinese exports' displacement dominate with regard to the ASEAN, but the complementary effect dominates with regard to the NIEs. It is now clear that China's competitive threat to ASEAN countries were overly exaggerated. As a processing and assembling centre, China sucks in a huge amount of parts and components and other categories of goods from the rest of East Asia, while the destinations of the final goods or processed and assembled goods are mainly developed countries, due to the specific position of the Chinese enterprises in the value chains of the international production network. The rest of East Asia dramatically improved their trade accounts rather than being wiped off the markets by their Chinese competitors. However, while the fear of China's competition by the rest of East Asia, the ASEAN countries in particular, is receding, the triangle trade imbalance among China, the rest of East Asia and the rest of world (the US in particular) has been worsening and has given rise to more and more concerns.

East Asian regional economic integration and the triangle imbalance

In 2003, according to the Chinese customs (Tables 5.5 and 5.6), China's trade surplus against the US was US$ 58.6 billion. At the same time, China's trade deficit against Japan, Korea, Taiwan and ASEAN 10 was 14.7 US$ billion, US$ 23 billion, US$ 29.1 billion and US$ 16.4 billion respectively, which adds up to a total trade deficit amounting to US$ 83.2 billion. Mainland China ran a US$ 65.2 billion trade surplus against Hong Kong. However, a very high proportion of mainland China's exports would be re-exported to the rest of the world, especially to the US. In any account, the triangle trade imbalance among China, the rest of East Asia and the rest of world (the US in particular) is very serious indeed. It is even more worrying that the imbalance is, to a large extent, a result of the current pattern of regional division of labour and that of global division of labour. In other words, it is structural rather than cyclical.

The triangle trade pattern among China, the rest of the East Asia, and the US is not sustainable. There are two most likely cases under which the trade pattern will collapse: either America is no longer able

Table 5.5   China's trade with the rest of East Asia, 2003

	Exports	Imports	Surplus
Hong Kong	762.87	111.19	651.68
Japan	594.23	741.51	–147.28
Korea	200.96	431.35	–230.38
Taiwan	90.05	381.08	–291.04
ASEAN	309.25	473.27	–164.01
Brunei	0.34	3.12	–2.78
Burma	9.08	1.70	7.38
Cambodia	2.95	0.26	2.69
Indonesia	44.81	57.48	–12.68
Laos	0.98	0.11	0.87
Malaysia	61.41	139.87	–78.46
Philippine	30.94	63.06	–32.12
Singapore	88.69	104.84	–16.15
Thailand	38.28	88.27	–49.99
Vietnam	31.79	14.56	17.23
Total	1957.36	2138.40	–181.04

Note: unit US$ 100 million.

Source: Inkyo Cheong, 'East Asian Economic Integration: Korea's Perspectives', Department of Economics, Inha University, Korea, 26 January 2005.

to absorb massive trade deficits, or China is no longer able to maintain a big trade surplus against the rest of the world and hence a big trade deficit against the rest of the East Asia. The first case is obvious to anybody. The second case is not necessarily so obvious to foreign observers. There are at least four factors that may contribute to China's failure to absorb trade deficit against the rest of East Asia. First, due to trade liberalization and China's economic growth, China's domestic markets have become the target of multinationals. Over the past decade, foreign-funded enterprises in China have never been the main creator of China's trade surplus. Now, due to the fact that foreign-funded enterprises are becoming less export-orientated, their contribution to China's trade surplus will become even smaller, at least in relative terms. Second, China is a resource-constrained economy. To sustain its growth, it will have to absorb an increasing amount of external resources, intermediates, and capital goods. For instance, China imported more than 90 million tons of crude oil in 2003; in the first two months of 2004, the import volume of crude oil already topped 20 million tons. It is estimated that in the next 20 years, the shortage of steel, copper, tin and many other raw materials in China will be huge,

Table 5.6   China' major trade partners, 2002–2004 (billion US$)

	Jan–May 2004	2003	2002
Top ten import economies			
1 Japan	36.66	74.15	53.47
2 EU	27.10	53.06	38.54
3 Chinese TW	25.07	49.36	38.06
4 ASEAN	23.90	47.33	31.2
5 Korea	23.95	43.13	28.57
6 US	19.13	33.86	27.23
7 Hong Kong	4.44	11.12	10.74
8 Russia	4.89	9.73	8.41
9 Australia	4.25	7.3	5.85
10 Brazil		5.84	
11 India	3.58		
12 Canada			3.63
Top ten export economies			
1 US	43.23	92.47	69.95
2 Hong Kong	34.79	76.29	58.47
3 EU	38.62	72.15	48.21
4 Japan	27.43	59.42	48.44
5 ASEAN	14.70	30.93	23.57
6 Korea	9.76	20.1	15.50
7 Chinese TW	4.78	9.0	6.59
8 Australia	3.02	6.26	4.59
9 Canada	2.80	6.03	4.30
10 Russia	2.75	5.63	3.52

and the shortage will only be compensated through imports. Third, following the increase in living standards, both China's net savings and cheap labour-based competitiveness against other poorer countries will fall. Last but not least, outflows of investment incomes from China will increase, due to China's huge cumulated FDI stock that has amounted to US$ 500 billion. Correspondingly, the outflows of investment incomes will increase to a very high scale. Unfortunately, no reliable statistics can tell us how much profit FFEs have earned and how much investment incomes may flow out of China in the future. In any case, it is very likely that China will be forced to take action to reduce its trade deficit against the rest of East Asia. In short, when the US takes action to balance its current account in the near future and/or China takes action in response to the American adjustment or as a result of its own problems in a more remote future, the trade and FDI pattern in the region is bound to suffer a big blow. In other words, the current trade and FDI pattern in the East Asian region is not sustainable.

China's policy toward regional economic integration

After examining China's trade and investment relationship with the rest of East Asia, we can conclude that on the one hand, China's economic integration in the region has indeed gone a long way. On the other hand, China's economic relationship with the US and Europe is also very strong, if not stronger. At least in terms of export markets, the US is the most important of all. From a pure market point of view, it seems that there is no obvious reason why regional economic integration should be a goal China has to pursue. As a matter of fact, before the Asian financial crisis, apart from the great Chinese economic integration, the issue of economic integration in East Asia was not high on China's agenda. Only after the Asian Financial Crisis has regional economic integration attracted great attention in China.

The crux of China's external economic policy is trade liberalization within the WTO framework. China's main obligations as a WTO member consist of tariff reduction, the removal of quotas, dismantling NTB, opening up the telecommunication and financial services and other sectors. China has been faithfully implementing its WTO commitments since its entry into the organization in December 2001. China's economic reform and opening up was closely related to trade and investment with Hong Kong, Macao, Taiwan and neighbouring countries. However, up until the Asian financial crisis, China did not have a clear policy towards regional economic integration. The dominant factor in the pursuit of regional economic integration is geopolitic rather than economic. China was more used to dealing with its economic partners on a bilateral basis for fear of losing control over the process in which it was involved.

Financial cooperation in the East Asian region

After the Asian financial crisis, China was shocked by the powerful contagion effect of the crisis and came to realize the fact that the East Asian region, to a large extent, is a whole: when one country falls, its neighbours will fall. After the initial hesitation, the Chinese government has been actively involved in the regional financial cooperation in the East Asian region. The East Asian financial cooperation can be roughly divided into two parts: the creation of a regional financial architecture, and the management of regional exchange rate arrangements. According to Articles (Article 1) of Agreement of the International Monetary Fund, the IMF has six main functions. Among them the most important functions are the third function and the fifth function. The third function is to promote exchange stability, to maintain orderly exchange arrangements among members, and to avoid competitive exchange depreciation. The fifth function is to give confidence to members by making the general resources of the Fund temporarily available to them under adequate safeguards, thus providing them with an opportunity to correct maladjustments in their balance of payments without resorting to measures destructive of national or international prosperity. Correspondingly, the main functions of an East Asian financial architecture should include exchange of information, promoting transparency and, especially, providing rescue packages to the regional members.

The stillbirth of the AMF is attributable not only to the objection by the US and the IMF, but also to miscommunication or the lack of communication among some East Asian economies, including China. The process of establishing an East Asian financial architecture is a process of trust building, which should start from some less grandiose endeavours and then forge ahead gradually. Only when progress in easier but nonetheless serious cooperation has been made, can trust be created and consolidated. Before institutionalizing the regional monetary and financial integration, there are many less controversial and less irretrievable steps that can be taken.

The 'Chiang Mai Initiative' (CMI) is the most important milestone of the Asian financial crisis. According to The Joint Ministerial Statement of the ASEAN + 3 Financial Ministers Meeting, published on 6 May 2000, Chiang Mai, Thailand, the ASEAN + 3 agreed to strengthen policy dialogues and regional cooperation activities in the areas of capital flows monitoring, self-help and support mechanisms, and international financial reforms. They recognized a need to establish a regional financing arrangement to supplement the existing international facilities. They agreed to establish a network of research and training institutions to conduct research and training on issues of mutual interest. Besides these general statements, the statement declared that the 'Chiang Mai Initiative' involves an expanded ASEAN Swap Arrangement that would include ASEAN counties, and a network of bilateral swap and repurchase agreement facilities among ASEAN countries, China, Japan and the Republic of Korea. As of June 2004, 16 bilateral swap arrangements totalling US$ 36.5 billion have been signed. The swap arrangement marked an important turning point in the road for Asian financial cooperation in history. Recently, ASEAN + 3 ministers decided to review the main principles of CMI to enhance its effectiveness. Issues have been discussed such as how the swap arrangement based on bilateral agreements should be developed into one based on multilateral agreements, how to strengthen surveillance and relationship with IMF programmes, and so on. Another pillar in the Asian financial architecture is the development of an Asian bond market. In November 2002 the Asian Bond Market Initiative (ABMI) was launched. The ABMI aims to develop efficient and liquid bond markets in Asia, which would enable better utilization of Asian savings for Asian investments. The ABMI would also contribute to the mitigation of currency and maturity mismatches in financing. In recent years, important progress has been made in bond issuance in local currency.

Another important aspect of Asian financial cooperation is the coordination of exchange rate arrangements in the region. During and after the Asian financial crisis, the Chinese monetary authorities have maintained the stability of the RMB, which contributed greatly to the recovery of East Asian economies. As pointed out by McKinnon and Ohno (2000), if China were to let the Yuan begin depreciating, no sustainable equilibrium for the East Asian economy would exist. In other words, competitive devaluation in East Asia would be unavoidable and the crisis would have been much worse.

Asian counties' experience shows that the fixed exchange rate regime tends to invite speculative attacks, which would lead to a bigger instability in currency than under a free-floating exchange rate regime. However, due to lack of flexibility in the economic structure, a less developed country needs a stable currency. Therefore, to choose a middle way – to peg national currency to a basket of reserve currencies seems a favourable solution.

Many Chinese economists hope that based on the progress in CMI and ABMI, and on an East Asian exchange rate arrangement, a solid foundation for an Asian monetary union can be established in the future. The force behind the movement towards an Asian Monetary Union should be strong enough. First, it will facilitate and consolidate the progress made in regional trade liberalization and economic integration. Second, it will lead to the end of dollar domination of the international monetary system. The most important characteristic of the current international monetary system is the domination of the dollar. With the US dollar as the single most important international reserve money, the US is able to pay its huge current account deficits and to accumulate huge foreign debts. East Asian economies as a whole now hold more than US $1.6 trillion with very low returns. East Asians should stop footing the bills for spendthrift American households and use their own saving for investment in the region.

China's policy towards FTA in the region

In order of depth, economic integration can take the forms of free-trade area, customs union, common market, economic union and full integration. In Europe, there are two forms of integration: European Community (EC) and European Free Trade Area (EFTA). The EC integration experienced several stages: it started from a customs union (1968–1985), then became a common market (1985–now), and ended up as economic and monetary union with a common currency (1999–now). EFTA began as a FTA and has remained as such ever since. The creation of an economic integration process is a political rather an economic decision. Economic preconditions for an economic integration are important in shaping the characteristics of an economic integration but economic elements are not decisive. With adequate political will, necessary economic preconditions for initiating a process of economic integration can be created. In contrast, even if the economic relationship is already very close, without adequate political inputs, a closer economic relationship in the form of economic integration is impossible.

As mentioned earlier in this chapter, compared with the EC, economic conditions for a deep economic integration exist in East Asia. But the political will for achieving a full integration in the region is rather weak. Market force can provide incentives for governments in the region to take more actions to promote economic cooperation. However, traditional arguments for or against regional economic integration in terms of competitiveness and complementarity are not that important. Existing trade patterns and regional production networks are helpful but not decisive.

The key for an East Asian FTA is how far economic cooperation between China and Japan can go. The importance of the Sino–Japanese relationship to the East Asian FTA is as important as that of the German–Franco relationship to the EU. China and Japan are economically highly complementary. Unfortunately, historical problems and mutual distrust have become a stumbling block for a closer relationship. Populist politics are further damaging the relationship. Just two years ago, the mainstream politicians and economists in Japan were competing with each other to accuse China of exporting deflation. The attempt by Japanese politicians to force a RMB revaluation backfired and resulted in making a more flexible RMB regime more difficult.

Now, just one year after a warmer relationship, hostile attitudes have flashed up again in Japan. It is clear that, without a political agenda from the start, it is difficult for economies in the region to go very far in economic integration. It is difficult to image, if the German–Franco political relationship were in such poor shape and public sentiment toward each other in the two countries was so unstable, if not outright hostile, that the EC could have come into existence. It is beyond doubt that Japan will continue to maintain its special relationship with the US. It seems that Japanese leadership is determined to spend more time on formulating strategies to deal with the 'China threat', rather than promote Sino–Japanese economic cooperation, to say nothing of economic integration. On the other hand, China probably will continue to focus on Sino–American relations and warm up to Sino–European relations, while waiting for changes to happen in Japan. The prospect for Sino–Japanese economic integration is rather dim.

Besides the troublesome relationship with Japan, China's relationship with the rest of East Asia seems quite good. China will continue its policy towards trade liberalization and FDI attraction, with some adjustment within the WTO framework, and pursue trade liberalization in different areas at the same time.

After the Asian financial crisis, China has initiated the process of China + ASEAN 10 FTA. China will continue strenuously negotiating with its neighbouring countries (economic entities) and other countries to form various regional groupings to achieve trade liberalization.

Bilateral FTAs

FTAs have become fashionable among economic entities. FTAs are characterized by further reduction of tariffs and liberalization of service sectors. FTAs reflect WTO member countries' impatience with the slow pace of trade liberalization within the multilateral framework. FTAs signed include ASEAN FTA, ASEAN–Thailand ASEAN–Singapore, Japan–Singapore, China–Hong Kong, China–Macao; FTAs under negotiation include ASEAN–China, ASEAN–Japan, Korea–Japan, Korea–Singapore, Japan–Thailand, Japan–Malaysia and Japan–the Philippines. After the Asian financial crisis, China was still preoccupied by WTO accession and did not engage very actively in negotiating with other countries to form FTAs bilaterally. Japan is China's most important trading partner in the region. However, the possibility of the creation of a FTA with Japan still seems remote due to the huge gap between China and Japan's development levels, and political reasons, as mentioned above. From Japan's point of view, China's export of agricultural products would be a big problem for many Japanese farmers. For China, the value-add by concluding a FTA with Japan is obfuscated. China will reach out for any countries that are willing to negotiate with China for FTA, and distance will not be a problem.

Greater China FTA

Mainland China and Hong Kong Special Administrative Region have signed a sort of FTA, called 'Closer Economic Partnership Arrangements' (CEPA). It is also not unimaginable for Mainland China and Taiwan to form a FTA. The prospect for the creation of a FTA including Mainland China, Hong Kong, Macao and Taiwan is very promising. Despite the Taiwanese Administration's political posturing, the economic integration across the Taiwan Straits is already very deep indeed. The market force driving economic integration will be strong enough to lead to a full integration within the framework of Greater China in a not very distant future. The FTA and the final full integration will give a great impetus to regional economic integration in the East Asian region.

Trilateral FTAs

Some economists are arguing that China, Japan and Korea should form a trilateral FTA. Chinese economists are watching the negotiations between Japan and Korea carefully. China hopes that the FTA between Japan and Korea will not create discrimination against China. Some economists argue that under certain circumstances bilateral issues between two members might be better resolved on a trilateral basis. The argument seems plausible. China will be watchful on the negotiation between Japan and Korea and be willing to join in the trilateral discussions in due course.

Owing to the similarity in the levels of development and industrial structures, the competition between ASEAN and China is tense. However, the political relationship between China and ASEAN is very cordial. Because there is the necessity as well as goodwill, China and the ASEAN 10 have reached an FTA agreement. This is an important milestone. Even though there is a long way to go for China and ASEAN to complete the agreement, the ice has already been broken, the ship will move on.

Regional economic integration

China is both positive and realistic in promoting regional economic integration with the rest of East Asia. China does not and cannot have a grand plan for an Asian Economic Community. China has actively participated in regional cooperation in investment and trade cooperation and will continue to do so in the future. The China plus ASEAN 10 FTA, and Mainland China–Hong Kong FTA, and a Greater China FTA will contribute to the establishment of a region-wide FTA. It is worth mentioning that China is also actively engaged in other areas of regional economic integration. For example, in the field of financial cooperation China has been deeply involved in the establishment of a regional financial architecture that is complementary to the IMF since the Asian financial crisis. China has also participated in discussions with Japan, Korea and ASEAN 10 on exchange rate coordination in East Asia.

Multilateral trade liberalization

China's accession into the WTO is an epoch-making event for the Chinese economy. No one, even the most picky American trade officials, can accuse China of not being serious about its commitments. However, some of China's trade partners are abusing the safeguard measures and anti-dumping rules against China's exports. Different from general safeguard measures, the safeguard measures specially designed for China are stronger than America's article 201, the most severe measure of all. The condition for initiating the measures against Chinese exports is 'material injury', instead of 'serious injury'. The specific safeguard measures will be in place for 12 years after China's joins the WTO. China has also accepted the anti-dumping rules that were based on denying China's status as a market economy for the purpose of trade protection. After WTO entry, China will be treated as a non-market economy for 15 years. This in fact gives the American government (and other like-minded governments) the arbitrary power in deciding whether a given Chinese product is priced below the cost. Chinese exports are entirely at the mercy of American government and interest groups.

So far Chinese enterprises have been implicated in more than 600 cases of anti-dumping suits, which accounted for 15 per cent of world total. China has lost 70 per cent of its cases. The key for China's loss in legal battles is China's non-market economy status. This is an uttermost unfair characterization of the Chinese economy. Despite the fact that the Chinese public are sick and tired of the disputes, China will stick to its WTO commitments, no matter how unhappy the Chinese public opinions may be for the concessions made by the Chinese delegation during the negotiation for WTO entry. On the other hand,

Table 5.7   China's efforts in promoting East Asian economic integration

	Economies	Objectives and contents
Sub-regional		
China–Hong Kong: 29.6.2003; China–Macao 17.10.2003; 'Closer Economic Partnership Arrangements' (CEPA)	China–HKSAR; China–Macao SAR	Great China FTA. Gradually cut or eliminate virtually all tariffs on and NTBs to trade of goods; Gradually liberalize all trade of services; Gradually cut or eliminate virtually all discriminative measures on trade and investment between partners
Economic cooperation in great Mekong river region; GMS (1992)	China, Burma, Laos, Thailand, Cambodia and Vietnam	Transportation, agriculture and forestry, water and electricity, minerals, tourisms, bio-resources, human resources, adjustment of industrial structure, environmental protection, construction of economic corridor, and trade and investment facilitation
Pan-Asia Railway construction: a key project in the development of Mekong river area	China, Burma, Laos, Thailand, Cambodia, Vietnam, Malaysia and Singapore	East Line: from Kunming via Hanoi; central line: from Kuming through Laos to Singapore; West Line: from Dali via Burma to Singapore
Development of North-East and Bohai rim	China, Japan, Korea, PDK, Mongolia and Russia	Around Japan Sea local governments summit, China, Japan and Korea tripartite FTA negotiations, Northeast Development Bank, Pan Yellow Sea economic and technological exchanges, the Development of Tumen river area (energy, transportation and communication, environment, tourism and education)

Table 5.7 China's efforts in promoting East Asian economic integration –
continued

	Economies	Objectives and contents
Bilateral and multilateral		
G3	China, Japan and Korea	Trilateral FTA. Mechanism of regular summit meetings; Ministerial conferences in areas of diplomacy, economics and trade, finance, environment, information and communication, patents and so on; other high level meetings in areas of trade and investment, information and communications, environment protection, disaster prevention and relief, energy cooperation, finance, science and technology, tourism, fishery, personnel exchanges, culture, education, development of human resources, news media, public health, sports and so on
ASEAN+1	ASEAN and China	ASEAN–China FTA. 10+1 summit meetings; 10+1 ministerial meetings in areas of diplomacy, economics and trade, finance, and transportation and communication, and so on. 10+1 high level economic officials; China–ASEAN Economic and Trade Cooperation Joined Committee; Expert Group of China–ASEAN Economic Cooperation; 10+1 Macroeconomic Forum; 10+1 Cooperation Forum Conference

Table 5.7 China's efforts in promoting East Asian economic integration – *continued*

Economies		Objectives and contents
ASEAN+3	ASEAN + China, Japan and Korea	10+3 summit meetings; 10+3 ministerial meetings in areas of diplomacy, economics and trade, finance, environment, tourism and so on; 10+3 high level economic officials; 10+3 high ranking official working group meetings on exchanges and cooperation in trade, investment, finance, IT tech, environment protection, flows of goods, energy, anti-terrorism, and non-traditional security.

China will contest any unjustified charges of injury and dumping vigorously. Trade disputes with the US and some European countries may provide China with an extra impetus to strength its economic cooperation with the rest of East Asia.

Table 5.7 is a summary of what China has done and is doing in promoting regional economic integration.

Concluding remarks

Realizing full regional economic integration in East Asia is in the interests of all countries and economies in the region. The economies in the region have gone a long way towards regional economic integration. To a large extent, the deepening of economic cooperation is market-driven. The economic foundation in East Asia for achieving the goal of regional economic integration is much more solid than in Europe when the European Community initiative was launched. However, due to the lack of political will for achieving the goal of economic integration in the region, institution building for the purpose of regional economic integration is scarce and largely cosmetic, as opposed to what the EU countries had done from the start of the process of economic integration. Therefore, the prospect for an East Asian Economic Community is not very encouraging.

Asian leaders must take a gradualist approach towards an EAEC. Only when market forces further drive the countries in the region to come closer, circumstances provide expected or unexpected impetus for the integration (such as another Asian financial crisis), all the pieces that have been made in the past come together, and, most importantly, peoples in the region change their perceptions of their neighbours, then can the dream of East Asian economic integration have a chance to come true.

While we should not pretend that the momentum of economic integration in East Asia is very strong and the goal of economic integration will be achieved in one or two generations, no efforts should be spared to promote the process of economic integration. Efforts in regional financial cooperation and FTA negotiations are highly recommended. As long as we keep going, the goal of regional economic integration will be kept alive. Where there is a will, there is a way. Let's 'hope', not just 'wait'.

References

Akamatsu, K. (1943) 'Shinkou Kogyokoku no Sangyo Hatten' (Industrial Development in Newly Industrializing Countries), in Ueda Teijiro-hakusi Kinen Ronbunshu (*Essays in Honor to Dr Teijiro Ueda*), Kagakushugi Kogyosha, Tokyo, Vol. 4.

Ando, M. and F. Kimura (2003) 'Formation of production and distribution networks in East Asia', NBER annual East Asia conference.

Athukorala, P.-C. (2003) 'Product fragmentation and trade pattern in East Asia', Trade and Development discussion paper 2003/21, Division of Economics, Research School of Pacific and Asian Studies, The Australian National University, Canberra.

Lee, Chang Jae, 'Rationale for institutionalizing North East Asian economic cooperation and some possible options', in Strengthening Economic Cooperation in Northeast Asia, Korea Institute of International Economic Policy (KIEP), September 2004, pp. 16–45.

Deardorff, A. V. (1998) 'Fragmentation in simple trade models', Paper 98–11, Michigan: Center for Research on Economic & Social Theory.

Development Research Centre of the State Council (2003) 'Analysis of China's processing trade and industrialization', *Economic Reference Materials*, 6 (www.drc.gov.cn).

Frankel, J. A. and A. K. Rose (1996) 'Economic structure and the decision to adopt a common currency', CIDER Working Paper No. C96–073, University of California at Berkley.

Fukao, K. H. Ishido and K. Ito (2003) 'Vertical intra-industrial trade and direct investment in East Asia', RIETI discussion paper 03-E-001.

Kiss, E. F. (2000) *Optimum Currency Area: Euro as a Practical Paradigm?* Rutgers, the State University of New Jersey.

Kojima, K. (1973) 'Reorganization of north-south trade: Japanese model of multinational business operation', *Hitotsubashi Journal of Economics*, 13(2), 1–28.

Krugman, P. (2004) 'The "new" economic geography: where are we?', Paper presented at the IED-JETRO symposium, 26 November.

Kuroda, K. (2000) *The Rise of China and the Changing Industrial Map of Asia*, Japan Economic Foundation.

McKinnon, R. I. (1998) 'Exchange rate coordination for surmounting the East Asian currency crisis', *Asian Economic Journal*, 12(4), December.

McKinnon, R. I. (2000) 'After the crisis, the East Asian dollar standard resurrected: An interpretation of high-frequency exchange rate pegging', Economic Department, Stanford University, online at: mckinnon@leland.stanford.edu

McKinnon, R. I. and K. Ohno (1997) *Dollar and Yen*, Cambridge, MA: The MIT Press.

Radelet, S. and J. D. Sachs (1998) 'The East Asian financial crisis: Diagnoses, remedies, prospects', *Brookings Papers on Economic Activity* 1.

Sakakibara, E. and S. Yamakawa (2004) 'Market-driven regional integration in East Asia', Paper for the workshop on 'Regional economic integration in a global framework', 22–23 September, Beijing.

The Nikkei Weekly (2001) 'PC makers rethink as slowdown hits', *The Nikkei Weekly*, 23 July, p. 18.

Trivisvavet, T. (2001) 'Do East Asian countries constitute an optimum currency area?', Durham University. April.

UNCTAD (2001) *Trade and Development Report, 2001*, Geneva: UNCTAD.

Vernon, R. (1964) 'International investment and international trade in the product cycle', *Quarterly Journal of Economics*, 80(2), 190–207.

Yamazawa, I. (1990) 'Economic development and international trade', East–West Center, RSI, Hawaii.

Yu, Y. (2000) 'China's deflation during the Asian financial crisis, and reform of the international financial system', *Asian Economic Bulletin* 17(2), August, 163–74.

Yu, Y. (2000) 'China: The case for capital controls', in W. Bello, N. Bullard and K. Malhotra (eds), *Global Finance*, London and New York: Zed Books, 177–87.

Zhang, Z. (2000) 'Exchange rate reform in China: An experiment in the real targets approach', *The World Economy*, 23(8), 1057–82, Oxford: Blackwell Publishers.

6
Regional Integration from a Korean Perspective*

Young-Han Kim

Introduction

With the launch of official negotiations on the Korea–Japan Free Trade Agreement in 2003, a deluge of discussions and policy suggestions are provided over the future direction of FTA formation in the Asian region from the perspective of Korea, as a country with an intermediate technology and an intermediate market size. The current Korean government gives first priority to the formation of the bilateral FTA with Japan followed by the FTA with ASEAN and other Asian countries while China remains as a partner in the future, not in the near future. Regarding the above Korean government approach, many criticisms are raised especially from the long-term industrial restructuring aspects.

One argument goes that when Korea forms a FTA with Japan excluding all the other Asian counties, Korean industrial structure, which is vertically integrated to the Japanese industries in terms of technology, might specialize in less valued-added sectors, where she has comparative advantage compared to Japan. A counter-argument goes that with the larger market access chances and the increased competition with Japan, the efficiency of the Korean economy will be enhanced. Without theoretical consensus on the long-term industrial effects of the Korea–Japan exclusive bilateral FTA, the Korean government intended to launch the agreement. However, lately, the more-in-depth analysis on the industrial effects of bilateral FTA have been emphasized.[1] The arguments on the long-term industrial effects of the Korea–Japan FTA can be generalized as the issue of the preferential trade agreement's long-term effects between the technologically asymmetric countries. This chapter examines this controversial issue focusing on the impacts of technical asymmetry on the FTA's welfare effects and the optimal path of regional integration in the Asian region considering the technological asymmetry.

The dynamic path to reach Asian economic integration can be categorized into three groups: i) Sequential bilateral trade agreement initiated by the Korea–Japan FTA followed by Korea's FTA with other Asian countries; ii) Hub and spoke type FTA, i.e., simultaneous multiple bilateral FTAs; and iii) a multilateral FTA such as a Pan-Asia wide FTA. This chapter examines the welfare effects and the producer surplus effects of each case, and determines the optimal path for a country with intermediate technology such as Korea.

There have been several approaches to examine the economic impacts of forming preferential trade agreement, and prior studies can be categorized into three groups. The first group, based on simulations about the impacts of FTA formation through a computable general equilibrium (CGE) model, tried to provide a projection on the static effects on trade balance and other macroeconomic variables.[2] The second group of studies focuses on the coalition formation issue based on the incentive mechanism to abide by the FTA arrangement. Through this analytical model based approach, attempts were made to examine whether a FTA is a stumbling bloc or a stepping-stone towards multilateral trade liberalization. The third approach is led by economic geographic approaches with special emphasis on the spatial economy.[3] This approach has its strong points in examining the industrial agglomeration and relocation effect of a FTA.

Regarding the economic impacts of FTA in the Asian region, most studies took the first approach, which is to estimate the impact of removing tariff barriers between FTA member countries based on a computable general equilibrium model. It is well known that the CGE approach has several shortcomings caused by its static approach in addition to too strong assumptions such as perfectly competitive markets and the constant returns to scale in the production technology. Even with these shortcomings of CGE approaches, there have been few trials to provide comprehensive analytic model analysis on FTA issues in Asia.

There are several representative prior researches, which can be categorized as a second group of FTA analyses focusing on coalition formation, and policy coordination incentive issues based on analytic model, although none of them pay special attention to the Asian region. Grossman and Helpman (1995) examine the conditions for the benefit from FTA to be larger than the loss in import competing industries. They assume two small countries with no market power. A policy with respect to FTA formation issues is decided to maximize the political objective function, while the aggregate welfare of voters is given by the summation of the aggregate labour supply, firms' profit, tariff revenue and consumer surplus. The government's objective function is the summation of firms' political contributions and the weighted aggregate welfare. Based on these assumptions, Grossman and Helpman examine the condition for the government's support for the FTA, and demonstrate that FTA is supported when enhanced protection is more likely, which deteriorates social welfare.

Bagwell and Staiger (1997) show that the formation of a FTA between symmetric countries tends to increase tariff levels temporarily to reduce the incentive to deviate from the tariff cooperation based on the self-enforcing mechanism during the transition period. However, custom union tends to decrease the temporary tariff level because of the market power effect. Krishna (1998) argues that a trade-diverting preferential agreement is more likely to be supported politically, and such preferential arrangements could critically change domestic incentives. So multilateral liberalization could be rendered infeasible by preferential arrangement. Freund (2000) shows that as the multilateral tariff was lowered, it is more likely that the tariff cooperation for FTA is sustained.

The prior studies provided much progress in understanding the welfare effects of FTA formation and dynamic incentive issues. However, most of them were based on the assumption of symmetric countries with complete information assumption. The North East Asian region, composed of Korea, Japan and China, is characterized by sharp differences in the technology levels and market size. In addition, information about each country's technology level and government's indirect influences on corporate sectors are not fully shared with each other country.

With these backgrounds, this chapter examines the effects of technology asymmetry on the welfare level of a FTA member country, and the optimal dynamic path of FTA formation among technologically asymmetric countries. Based on a simple model of four countries with linear demand functions and differentiated products, this chapter demonstrates that the optimal path of regional integration for the country with an intermediate technology level would be to form multiple bilateral FTAs, i.e., Hub and spoke type FTA between technically asymmetric countries from the very initial stage. The second best regime is the multilateral Asia-wide FTA. The worst case for a country with an intermediate technology would be to form a FTA with a country with advanced technologies, and extends the FTA with the less developed countries in the later stage. These results imply that the

optimal strategy of regional integration for a country with an intermediate technology level, such as Korea, is to form a Hub and spoke type
FTA rather than a bilateral FTA with Japan followed by the participation of other Asian countries.

This chapter is organized as follows. The next section discusses the
recent development and challenges of regional integration from the perspective of Korea. The theoretical model is described in the following
section, focusing on the case of FTA formation between symmetric countries as a benchmark discussion. We then examine the influences of technology asymmetry on the welfare level of each country and determine
the optimal path of regional economic integration based on the welfare
analysis. The fifth section discusses policy implications and concludes.

The recent development and challenges of regional integration from the perspective of Korea

With the rapid development of regional integration worldwide led by
the US and EU, the Korean government changed its traditional policy
orientation based on multilateralism toward regionalism worrying
about the possibility that Korea might be left out from the world-wide
trends of preferential market opening. Based on the understanding that
participation in the preferential trade agreement is an inescapable and
urgently required policy tool for foreign market access and sustainable
growth, the Korean government has actively pursued FTA arrangements. Recently, the bilateral FTAs with Chile, Singapore and EFTA were
activated, and numerous FTA negotiations are undergoing including
Korea–US FTA and Korea–Canada FTA.

At the initial stage of the Korean government's efforts for FTA formation, the basic policy objective could be described as the maximization
of the number of FTA agreements. Therefore, the preferred FTA partner
countries for Korea were the countries with the least political barriers to
reaching a final agreement. As had already been demonstrated at the
Cancun DDA meeting in 2003, the agricultural sector is one of the most
actively organized interests group against domestic market opening in
Korea. Therefore, the Korean government started FTA negotiations with
the partner countries that impose least threat on agricultural market
opening, such as Japan, Singapore, and Chile.[4] Therefore, the traditional
Korean government approach could be described as the sequential
FTA strategy, i.e., Korea–Japan FTA as the first FTA with the major
trading partner followed by other Asian countries such as ASEAN, and
China. However, lately, some changes can be observed in government

approaches toward FTA formation with the understanding that FTA formation has the same effect as the industrial restructuring policy. So, to minimize the possible industrial distortion effect and maximize the foreign market access chances, the Korean government announced its FTA policy direction as 'the simultaneous bilateral FTA formation'.

The major challenges of Asian regional integration from the perspective of Korea

Participation in Asian regional integration under the form of FTA is expected to provide the Korean economy with trade creation effects and also investment creation effects in addition to the additional market access chances. However, one important characteristic of the Asian regional integration is that it is integration between technically sharply asymmetric countries. Traditionally, the Asian industrial structure has been characterized as 'the flying geese', led by the Japanese high-end technologies with the Asian NIES playing the middle parts, and the other Asian countries flying at the back with relatively low level technologies.

Recent studies on the technology gap between Japan and Korea show that technological dependence of Korean industries on Japanese core technologies is deepened, especially great in high-tech telecommunication industries. For example, Japanese parts and component takes 53 per cent of total value-added (TVA) of Korean mobile phones, and 38 per cent of TVA of the general electronic goods including household electronic goods. Korean industries are deeply worried about the possibility that if a Korea–Japan FTA is launched for a first Korean FTA with a major trading partner followed by FTAs with other Asian countries with a significant time gap, it is highly likely that Korean industries will specialize in the sectors with comparative advantage compared to Japan, such as textile industry, IT assembly industries based on Japanese core components, and mass production process with low value-adding technologies. Based on the above backgrounds, it is argued that Korean industries' specialization in the sectors with comparative advantage in lower-level technologies through a Korea–Japan FTA will enhance the efficiency of resource allocation and the welfare of Korea only when the Korea–Japan FTA is accompanied with the proper capital and technology transfer within the region. Otherwise, the bilateral FTA between Korea and Japan, which will induce Korean industries to specialize in low-value adding sectors, will result in the rapid collapse of the Korean industrial base in the high-value adding sectors, leading to serious deterioration of macroeconomic performance.

An analysis of the welfare effects of three different types of FTA formation between technically asymmetric countries based on a simple oligopoly model where representative firms with asymmetric technology from each country compete in Cournot fashion shows the following results. When Korea takes the sequential FTA strategy, i.e., first a Korea–Japan FTA followed by a Korea–ASEAN FTA and then a Korea–China FTA with a significant time gap, the producer surplus of the country with an intermediate technology level, in this case Korea, is decreased. Hub and spoke type FTA strategy, where Korea forms multiple bilateral FTAs Korea–Japan FTA. Korea–ASEAN FTA and Korea–China FTA simultaneously, Korean social welfare and producer surplus will be significantly increased. The welfare effect of multilateral FTA arrangement, that is to form Korea–China– Japan FTA from the initial stage, turns out to be lower than that of the hub and spoke type FTA, however, still higher than that from the Sequential FTA strategy. The simulation results with the actual data on the technology gap show that Korean producer surplus decreases 20.16 per cent from the sequential FTA strategy while it increases 11.48 per cent from the hub and spoke type FTA strategy. Table 6.1 shows the technology gaps between Japan and Korea.

Future tasks and policy implications of regional integration in East Asia from the Korean perspective

As discussed in the previous section, while the Korea–Japan FTA is under negotiation, Korean industries are worried about the possibility

Table 6.1 Technology competitiveness of Japanese industries compared with the Korean technology level

	Design technology	R&D technology	Production technology	Product quality	General technology	Technology gap (years)
Semiconductor	108.6	106.8	100.0	104.0	104.9	0.8
Computer	106.3	112.0	101.0	104.0	105.8	1.7
Shipbuilding	107.3	108.0	108.8	101.7	106.5	0.6
Household Electronics	107.8	108.3	102.8	107.8	106.7	1.4
Textiles	108.2	116.0	106.0	110.2	110.1	1.8
Telecommunication Equipments	116.2	109.4	104.6	111.0	110.3	1.3
Petrochemicals	119.5	117.8	106.8	105.0	112.3	3.1
Steel Industries	116.9	113.8	115.1	116.8	115.7	3.2
Motor Vehicles	117.9	114.1	114.6	117.9	116.1	3.0
General Machines	120.7	120.7	112.7	115.0	117.3	5.5

Note: Korean technology level = 100.
Sources: Korea Bank of Industries, *Survey on Korean Technologies*, 2004.

that Korean industries might specialize in the sectors with comparative advantage such as low-value added mass production sectors while technology intensive sectors might agglomerate to Japan, where there are strong backward and forward linkage effects in the high-tech industries. The Chinese strategy of Asian regional integration mainly from the southern part of China such as ASEAN and not giving high priority to integration with Japan might be understood in the same context. Moreover, recent territorial tensions and other historical and cultural factors work as barriers against upcoming East Asian economic integration.

The model

Assume that four countries with asymmetric technologies consider the formation of preferential trade agreements among them. Country A is assumed to have the most advanced technologies, i.e., has the lowest marginal cost to produce the same unit value output compared to other competing counties. Country B is assumed to have the intermediate level of technologies while countries C and D have the lowest level of technologies, i.e., the highest marginal cost: $c_A < c_B < c_C = c_D$. To focus on the impacts of asymmetric technologies, we assume that the market size and the consumer utility structure of each country are symmetric. The inverse demand function of each country is defined as follows: $P_i = a - bQ_i$ where $i = A, B, C, D$ and Q_i is the total quantity demanded in market i. There is one representative firm in each country. The inverse demand function in country A is given as follows:

$$P_A = a - b(q_A + \chi_{BA} + \chi_{CA} + \chi_{DA})$$

where q_A is the output of firm A for the home market and x_{BA} is the output produced by the firm in country B to export to country A.

The profit function of firm A under MFN regime with no preferential agreement is described as:

$$\Pi_A = (P_A - c_A)\, q_A + (P_B - c_A - t_B)\chi_{AB} + (P_C - c_A - t_C)\chi_{AC} + \qquad (1)$$
$$(P_D - c_A - t_D)\chi_{AD}$$

where c_A is the marginal production cost of firm A, and t_i is the import tariff imposed by country i.

The inverse demand functions and the profit functions for B, C, and D are defined in the same way respectively. The government of each country decides its trade policy, i.e., FTA formation strategy and the import tariff level, and then each firm decides its output strategy after it observes the trade policies. In this two-stage game, market equilibrium can be obtained by backward induction.

The welfare effects of MFN regime between technically asymmetric countries as a benchmark discussion

To examine the welfare effects of various types of FTA formation between technologically asymmetric countries, we check the case of MFN-type regime with no preferential trade agreement among four countries as a benchmark discussion.[5] When each country's trade policy is decided according to the MFN (Most Favoured Nation) principle with no preferential agreement, the equilibrium tariffs of country A, B, C and D under the simultaneous decision-making process are decided in the following way. By backward induction, the equilibrium output of the firm in each country is determined first. The best response functions of firm A in each market are derived from the profit maximization problem with respect to output levels as strategic variables. The best response functions of firms B, C and D are derived in the same way. Moreover, to simplify the notation, we assume the technology differences between the countries are symmetric in the following sense: $c_A = c - \gamma$, $c_B = c$, $c_C = c_D = c + \gamma$, while $\gamma > 0$. Then, the four representative firms' equilibrium outputs in country A are obtained by solving four firms' reaction functions in country A simultaneously:

$$q_A = \frac{a - c + 6\gamma + 3t_A}{5b}, \quad \chi_{BA} = \frac{a - c + \gamma - 2t_A}{5b}, \quad (2)$$

$$\chi_{CA} = \frac{a - c - 4\gamma - 2t_A}{5b}, \quad \chi_{DA} = \frac{a - c - 4\gamma - 2t_A}{5b}$$

With asymmetric technologies and symmetric demand functions, the equilibrium output in countries B, C and D are respectively:

$$q_B = \frac{a - c + \gamma + 3t_B}{5b}, \quad \chi_{AB} = \frac{a - c + 6\gamma - 2t_B}{5b},$$

$$\chi_{CB} = \frac{a - c - 4\gamma - 2t_B}{5b}, \quad \chi_{DB} = \frac{a - c - 4\gamma - 2t_B}{5b}$$

$$q_C = \frac{a - c + 4\gamma + 3t_C}{5b}, \quad \chi_{AC} = \frac{a - c + 6\gamma - 2t_C}{5b}, \quad (3)$$

$$\chi_{BC} = \frac{a - c + \gamma - 2t_C}{5b}, \quad \chi_{DC} = \frac{a - c - 4\gamma - 2t_C}{5b}$$

$$q_D = \frac{a - c - 4\gamma + 3t_D}{5b}, \quad \chi_{AD} = \frac{a - c + 6\gamma - 2t_D}{5b},$$

$$\chi_{BD} = \frac{a - c + \gamma - 2t_D}{5b}, \quad \chi_{CD} = \frac{a - c - 4\gamma - 2t_D}{5b}$$

The social welfare function of country A is defined as the sum of the consumer surplus, the producer surplus, and the government surplus, i.e., the import tariff revenue:

$$SW = CS + PS + GS = \int_{p*}^{a} D(P)dP + \prod_{AA} + \prod_{AB} + \prod_{AC} + \qquad (4)$$
$$\prod_{AD} + t(\chi_{BA} + \chi_{CA} + \chi_{DA})$$

With the continuously quasi-concave well-behaving social welfare function, the optimal trade policy for country A under the MFN trading regime is derived as a solution of the first order condition of the social welfare maximization problem with respect to the tariff as follows: $t_A^* = (9a - 9c + 4\gamma)/33$. Under the MFN trading regime, the social welfare of country A is obtained by substituting the equilibrium tariffs and equilibrium outputs into the social welfare functions respectively as follows:

$$SW_A(MFN) = \frac{54 + 891a^2 + 945c^2 - 198a(9c - 4\gamma) + 1488\gamma + 13457\gamma^2 - 12c(9 + 190\gamma)}{2178b}$$

In the same way, the equilibrium tariff and the welfare of country B are obtained as follows respectively: $t_B^* = (9 - 9c - \gamma)/33$,

$$SW_B(MFN) = \frac{927 + 18a^2 + 945c^2 + 18r + 506\gamma^2 - 6c(309 + 13\gamma) + a(-36c + 60\gamma)}{2178b}$$

Welfare analysis of different FTA formation strategies among technically asymmetric countries

The dynamic path of FTA formation in the Asian region can be categorized into three categories as follows: i) Sequential bilateral free trade agreements initiated by the Korea–Japan FTA followed by Korea's FTA with other Asian countries; ii) Hub and spoke type FTA, i.e., simultaneous multiple bilateral FTAs; and iii) a multilateral FTA such as a Pan-Asia wide FTA. The welfare effect of each scenario is examined in sequence. Three different paths of FTA formation produce different effects not only in static terms but in dynamic terms. Moreover, the dynamic effects amplify the static effects due to the economies of scale effects and the learning effects. In this section, to focus on the comparison of welfare effect of three different scenarios of FTA formation, the discussion is limited to the static effects of three different scenarios.

Equilibria of three different FTA formation strategies

When a country with an intermediate technology level (Country *B*) takes the strategy of forming a sequential bilateral FTA formation, first with a technologically advanced country (*A*) followed by the bilateral FTA with a lower-technology level country (*C*), the welfare effects of the strategy turns out as follows. The total of welfares of the sequential bilateral FTA formation can be obtained by summing up each stage's welfare, first, the welfare of bilateral FTA formation with country *A*, and second, the welfare of multiple bilateral FTAs stage such as the simultaneous bilateral FTA between *A* and *B* and *B* and *C*. We examine the first stage welfare, and add up with the second stage welfare.

In the first stage, when country *B* forms an exclusive FTA with country *A* excluding countries *C* and *D*, the equilibrium welfare is obtained by backward induction. First, the reaction functions of four representative firms are derived with the assumption that firms observe the formation bilateral FTA between country *A* and *B*, and then the firms' equilibrium outputs are obtained as solutions of four simultaneous equations of reaction functions. By substituting these equilibrium outputs into the welfare maximization problem of each country, the optimal trade policy for each country is obtained as follows:

$$t_A^* = \frac{3a - 3c + 7\gamma}{24}, \ t_B^* = \frac{3a - 3c + 17\gamma}{24}, \text{ and } t_C^* = \frac{3a - 3c + 2\gamma}{24}$$

The equilibrium welfare of each country is obtained as follows:

$$SW_A^* = \frac{1}{17424b}(1377 + 6534a^2 + 7911c^2 - 4356a(3c - \gamma) + 16050\gamma + 97951\gamma^2 - 6c(459 + 3401\gamma))$$

$$SW_B^* = \frac{1}{17424b}(6822 + 1089a^2 + 7911c^2 - 726a(3c - \gamma) - 2628\gamma + 12151\gamma^2 + 6c(-2274 + 317\gamma))$$

$$SW_C^* = \frac{1}{17424b}(3353 + 121a^2 + 3474c^2 - 4566\gamma + 2226\gamma^2 - 242a(c + 5\gamma) + 2c(-3353 + 2888\gamma))$$

Moreover, the equilibrium outputs of each country under the sequential bilateral FTA formation strategy turn out as follows:

$$q_A = \frac{a - c + 6\gamma + 2t_A}{5b}, \quad \chi_{BA} = \frac{a - c + \gamma + 2t_A}{5b},$$

$$\chi_{CA} = -\frac{-a + c + 4\gamma + 3t_A}{5b}, \quad \chi_{DA} = -\frac{-a + c + 4\gamma + 3t_A}{5b}$$

$$q_B = \frac{1 - c + \gamma + 2t_B}{5b}, \quad \chi_{AB} = \frac{1 - c + 6\gamma + 2t_B}{5b},$$

$$\chi_{CB} = -\frac{-1 + c + 4\gamma + 3t_B}{5b}, \quad \chi_{DB} = -\frac{-1 + c + 4\gamma + 3t_B}{5b}$$

$$q_C = \frac{-1 + c + 4\gamma - 3t_C}{5b}, \quad \chi_{AC} = \frac{-1 + c - 6\gamma + 2t_C}{5b},$$

$$\chi_{BC} = -\frac{1 - c + \gamma - 2t_C}{5b}, \quad \chi_{DC} = -\frac{-1 + c + 4\gamma + 2t_C}{5b}$$

$$q_D = \frac{-1 + c + 4\gamma - 3t_D}{5b}, \quad \chi_{AD} = \frac{-1 + c - 6\gamma + 2t_D}{5b},$$

$$\chi_{BD} = -\frac{1 - c + \gamma - 2t_D}{5b}, \quad \chi_{CD} = -\frac{-1 + c + 4\gamma + 2t_D}{5b}$$

The output of each firm in each market shows that with the sequential bilateral FTA formation, the producer from country *A* with a higher technology gains more from the FTA formation and the producer from country *B* with an intermediate level technology loses from the arrangement as shown in the sharp increase of the *A*'s market share in *B*'s market. These output effects are straightforwardly reflected in the following results of producer surplus change of three types of FTA formation. As shown in Figure 6.1, the producer surplus of an inter-

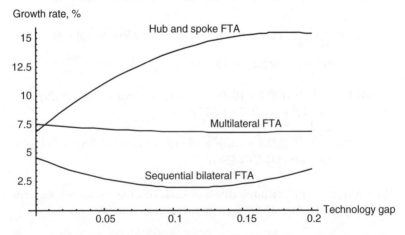

Figure 6.1 Social welfare effects of three FTA formation strategies to the country with an intermediate technology (country *B*)

mediate technology level is lowest in the case of sequential bilateral FTA, the decreases larger as the technology gap is increased.

When country *B* forms a multilateral FTA with countries *A* and *C*, so called the Grand FTA coalition, the tariffs between the countries *A*, *B* and *C* are removed while the tariff against the non-member country, country *D*, is decided by each country. Under the hub and spoke type FTA formation, country *B* arranges simultaneous bilateral FTAs with country *A* and country *C*. In this case, country *A* has no preferential market access to country *C* and vice versa. The equilibrium values of social welfare and the producer surplus in each case of FTA formation are provided in the Appendix 1.

Welfare effects of three different FTA formation strategies on the country with an intermediate level of technology (country *B*)

From the comparison of welfare effects in three different strategies of FTA formation, the welfare effects of the hub and spoke type FTA formation turns out to be highest for a country with an intermediate level of technology, followed by the Pan Asia-wide multilateral FTA formation strategy. The sequential bilateral FTA formation with a country with higher technology level produces the lowest welfare effects to a country with an intermediate technology level. The rationale behind

Table 6.2 Impacts on Korean industrial production of three FTA formation scenarios

	Sequential bilateral FTA	*Multilateral FTA*	*Hub and spoke type FTA*
Total Industries	–20.16%	–10.42%	11.48%
Semi-conductors (Non-memory)	–20.54%	–10.64%	10.82%
Computer	–16.13%	–8.26%	18.16%
Shipbuilding	–16.79%	–8.59%	17.11%
Household Electronics	–16.97%	–8.68%	16.81%
Textiles	–19.85%	–10.24%	12.01%
Telecommunication Equipments	–20.00%	–8.26%	16.97%
Petrochemicals	–21.49%	–11.21%	9.14%
Steel Industries	–12.65%	–10.64%	5.05%
Motor Vehicles	–23.93%	–12.81%	4.59%
General Machines	–24.65%	–13.30%	3.26%

Note: Estimation results of the model analysis based on the technology gap data from Korean Bank of Industries, 2004.

this result lies in that producer surplus effects shows a sharp contrast between the three strategies of FTA formation, basically in the same direction as the social welfare effects while consumer surplus effects are increased in the all three strategies. With the asymmetry between countries lying only in technologies while consumer preferences are symmetric, the welfare effects are decided by the impacts in the production sectors. The impact of the various FTA options in the case of Korea are shown in Table 6.2.

When we assume that the technology gap takes the feature of a 10 per cent difference in the marginal cost, the simulation results show that the hub and spoke type FTA formation increases the social welfare of the country with an intermediate technology (country B) by 13.8 per cent, while the multilateral FTA formation increases it by 6.9 per cent (see Table 6.3). The growth rate of social welfare from the sequential bilateral FTA formation is lowest at 2.0 per cent.

In the production sectors, when we assume that the marginal cost of country A is 10 per cent lower than that of country B, the hub and spoke type FTA formation increases the producer surplus of the country with an intermediate technology level by 12.1 per cent, while the multilateral FTA formation decreases it by 10.2 per cent. The producer surplus of country B is decreased most sharply in the case of the sequential FTA formation by 19.8 per cent. The intuition behind this result is that in case of hub and spoke type FTA formation, the country with an intermediate technology (country B) obtains a preferential market access that the country with a higher technology (country A) does not have. However, in case of multilateral FTA formation, the country with a higher technology obtains the same preferential market access chances as country B, which provides larger market share to country A while the domestic market share of country B is decreased.

Table 6.3   The impacts of three FTA formation strategies on country B

		Sequential bilateral FTA	Hub and spoke FTA	Multilateral FTA
Country with an intermediate technology (B)	Growth rate of social welfare (%)	2.01132	13.8156	6.88445
	Growth rate of producer surplus (%)	−19.7688	12.1471	−10.1981

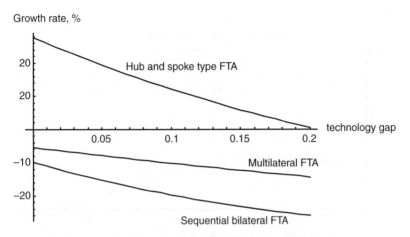

Figure 6.2 The producer surplus effects of FTA formation to country *B* with intermediate technology level

The industrial impact of the sequential bilateral FTA formation on country *B* is worst because it plays a losing game in terms of producer surplus with country *A* while the market access chance to country *C*, that is available in case of multilateral FTA formation, is no longer available.

Figure 6.2 shows the producer surplus effects of the various FTA types to country *B*.

The equilibrium producer surplus of each country under the sequential bilateral FTA formation strategy turns out as follows:

$$PS_A^* = \frac{54 + 891a^2 + 945c^2 - 198a(9c - 4\gamma) + 1488\gamma + 13457\gamma^2 - 12c(9 + 190\gamma)}{2178b}$$

$$PS_B^* = \frac{1377 + 1089a^2 + 2466c^2 - 726a(3c - \gamma) + 1002\gamma + 2834\gamma^2 - 54c(51 + 32\gamma)}{17424b}$$

The welfare effects of three FTA formation strategies on the country with a higher technology level (country *A*)

The welfare impacts of three FTA formation strategies are characterized by the complementarity effects of trade policies, in which each government tries to maximize its own social welfare considering the strategic interaction of the firms' output decision-making strategies and the each government's strategic policy decision-making process. The equilibria of three FTA formation strategies show that the social welfare level of the country with a higher technology is highest under the

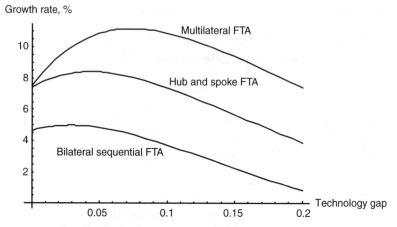

Growth rate, %

Figure 6.3   Social welfare impacts of FTA formation strategies on country *A*

multilateral FTA formation strategy. Hub and spoke FTA formation strategy provides a higher welfare level than the bilateral sequential FTA formation strategy to country *A* due to the complementarity effects caused by the increased number of countries which participate in the preferential trade arrangements (see Figure 6.3).

Policy implication and concluding remarks

This chapter examined the welfare effects of forming FTA between technologically asymmetric countries comparing three different paths of FTA formation. Based on a model analysis assuming symmetric preferences and markets size with four representative firms of each country competing in Cournot fashion, the chapter demonstrated that the optimal path of regional integration for the country with an intermediate technology level would be to form simultaneous and multiple bilateral FTAs, i.e., hub and spoke type FTA between technically asymmetric countries from the very initial stage. The second best regime is the multilateral Asia-wide FTA. The worst case for a country with an intermediate technology would be to form a FTA with a country with an advanced technology, and extend the FTA to less developed countries at a later stage. These results imply that the optimal strategy of regional integration for a country with an intermediate technology level, such as Korea, is to form a hub and spoke type FTA rather than a bilateral FTA with Japan followed by the participation of other Asian countries.

The above results imply that positive static effects on the producer surplus of a country with an intermediate level of technology is available only in the case of hub and spoke type FTA formation. Moreover, the static positive impacts from hub and spoke FTA formation might be amplified dynamically through the path of industrial agglomeration effect when the industries show strong forward and backward linkage effects. The same dynamic effects in addition to the industrial agglomeration effect will induce a sharp reduction of industrial sectors when the country with an intermediate country forms a sequential bilateral FTA starting with a partner country with a higher technology. Interpreting these results in geographic perspective provides the following message: When we assume South Korea as a country with an intermediate technology, the optimal strategy for South Korea to form FTA in the Asian region would be to take the hub and spoke FTA formation strategy, not a sequential FTA formation with Japan as a first FTA partner country followed by other Asian countries. Moreover, from the perspective of South Korea, it is welfare dominant that Korea forms separate bilateral FTAs with Japan and China to the case of trilateral FTA formation with Japan and China. The pre-requirement for the multiple bilateral FTAs is the fundamental industrial restructuring of Korean industries, such as reallocating the human and economic resources from the sectors of comparative disadvantage to the sectors with comparative advantage. The successful FTAs assumes nation-wide efforts involving the massive restructuring cost including the establishment of the social-safety net during the transition period.

Notwithstanding with strong message, this chapter should be extended in the following aspects to provide more realistic and feasible policy implications. First, further in-depth analysis on the effects of asymmetric market size and the asymmetric consumer preferences is required. In addition, to examining the dynamic effects and the relocation effect of industries after FTA formation, it is necessary to introduce a concrete production function incorporating the forward and backward linkage in the industries. These issues should be addressed in future studies.

Appendix A: the equilibria of three FTA formation strategies

The equilibrium values of social welfare that the country with intermediate technology level (country B) obtains are as follows:

SW_B(Sequential bilateral FTA) = $\dfrac{6822 + 1089a^2 + 7911c^2 - 726a(3c - r) - 2628r + 12151r^2 + 6c(-2274 + 317r)}{17424b}$

SW_B(Hub and spoke FTA) = $\dfrac{566449 + 88209a^2 + 654658c^2 - 58806a(3c - r) - 406364r - 407459r^2 + 2c(566449 + 232585r)}{1411344b}$

SW_B(Multilateral FTA) = $\dfrac{139105 + 15488a^2 + 154593c^2 - 7744a(4c - 3r) - 20598r + 105954r^2 + 2c(139105 + 1317r)}{331298b}$

In the same way, the equilibrium producer surplus of country B (country with an intermediate technology level) is obtained as follows:

PS_B(MFN) = $\dfrac{162 + 9a^2 + 171c^2 - 6a(3c - 5r) + 252r + 223r^2 - 6c(54 + 47r)}{1089b}$

PS_B(Sequential Bilateral FTA) = $\dfrac{1377 + 1089a^2 + 2466c^2 - 726a(3c - r) + 1002r + 2834r^2 - 54c(51 + 32r)}{17424b}$

PS_B(Hub and spoke FTA) = $\dfrac{194737 + 88209a^2 + 282946c^2 - 58806a(3c - r) + 133388r + 161725r^2 - 2c(194737 + 96097r)}{1411344b}$

PS_B(Multilateral FTA) = $\dfrac{16857 + 7744a^2 + 24601c^2 - 3872a(4c - 3r) + 19830r + 19097r^2 - 18c(1873 + 1747r)}{165649b}$

Country B's equilibrium consumer surplus is obtained as follows:

$$CS_A(\text{MFN}) = \frac{(-7 + 7c + 2r)^2}{242b}$$

$$CS_B(\text{Sequential Bilateral FTA}) = \frac{(9 - 9c + r)^2}{288b}$$

$$CS_B(\text{Hub and spoke FTA}) = \frac{2(10 - 10c + r)^2}{729b}$$

$$CS_B(\text{Multilateral FTA}) = \frac{(-29 + 29c + 4r)^2}{2738b}$$

Acknowledgements

Many valuable comments by Masahisa Fujita, Paul Krugman and Anthony Venables are deeply appreciated.

Notes

*   Reprinted and revised in part by permission of Elsevier from 'The optimal path of regional economic integration between asymmetric countries in the North East Asia' by Young-Han Kim, *Journal of Policy Modeling*, 27, pp. 673–87, 2005, by the Society for Policy Modeling.

1. See James and Movshuk (2003), Brown *et al.* (1996) and Yamazawa (2001) for the details of the economic and the political backgrounds of Korea-Japan FTA negotiation
2. The representative studies of CGE approaches include Hinojosa-Ojeda *et al.* (1999), Scollay and Gilbert (2000) and Brown *et al.* (1996).
3. The basic methodology and the major findings from economic geographic approaches are concisely summarized in Fujita *et al.* (1999).
4. Chile was believed to be as complementary agricultural country with respect to the Korean agricultural sector.
5. The Most Favoured Nation (MFN) clause, which is, as well known, the corner-stone of the WTO system, represents the trading system where all member countries are treated as the most favoured nation with no disadvantage compared to other member countries. That is, if one country is treated as a most favoured nation, the same treatment should be extended to the all member countries according to MFN clause. In this context, FTA formation is strictly contradictory to the MFN clause, the basic principle of WTO. However, the political realities where the leading countries in the WTO system are also the leaders in the formation of FTAs, comprise two conflicting features as in GATT's Article XXIV. See Hoekman and Kostecki (2001) for the detailed discussion on the relationship between the MFN clause and FTA formation.

References

Bagwell, K. and R. Staiger (1997) 'Multilateral tariff cooperation during the formation of free trade areas', *International Economic Review*, 38(2), 291–319.

Ballard, C. (1997) 'The effects of economic integration in the Pacific rim', *Journal of Asian Economics*, 8(4), 505–24.

Blecker, R. (1993) 'The new economic integration', *Regional Science & Urban Economics*, 23(3), 941–9.

Borvat, K. (1999) 'Third world regional integration', *European Economic Review*, 43(1), 47–64.

Brown, D., A. Deardorff and R. Stern (1996) 'Computational analysis of the economic effects of and East Asian preferential trading bloc', *Journal of Japanese and International Economies*, 10(1), 37–70.

Cadot, O., J. Melo and M. Olarreaga (2001) 'Can bilateralism ease the pains of multilateral trade liberalization?', *European Economic Review*, 45, 27–44.

Freund, C. (2000) 'Multilateralism and the endogenous formation of preferential trade agreements', *Journal of International Economics*, 52, 359–76.

Fujita, M., P. Krugman and A. Venables (1999) *The Spatial Economy: Cities, Regions, and International Trade*, Cambridge: MIT Press.

Garby, C. (1994) *Japan: A New Kind of Superpower?*, Washington: Woodrow Wilson Press.

Grossman, G. and E. Helpman (1995) 'The politics of free-trade agreements', *American Economic Review*, 85(4), 667–90.

Hanson, G. (1996) 'Economic integration, intra-industry trade, and frontier regions', *European Economic Review*, 40(3–5), 941–9.

Hinojosa-Ojeda, R., S. Robinson and F. De Paolis (1999) 'Regional integration among the unequal: A CGE model of NAFTA and the Central American Republics', *North American Journal of Economics and Finance*, 10(1), 235–92.

Hoekman, B. and M. Kostecki (2001) *The Political Economy of the World Trading System*, New York: Oxford University Press.

James, W. and O. Movshuk (2003) 'Comparative advantage in Japan, Korea and Taiwan between 1980 and 1999: Testing for convergence and implications for closer economic relations', *Developing Economies*, 41(3), 287–308.

Krishna, K. (1996) 'Market access and welfare effects of free trade areas without rules of origin', NBER Working Paper No. 5480.

Krishna, P. (1998) 'Regionalism and multilateralism: A political economy approach', *The Quarterly Journal of Economics*, February, 227–51.

Krueger, A. (1995) 'Free trade agreements versus custom unions', *NBER Working Paper* No. 5084.

Lewis, J. (1995) 'Beyond the Uruguay round: The implication of an Asian free trade area', *China Economic Review*, 35–90.

Lloyd, P. (1992) 'Regionalization and world trade', *OECD Economic Studies*, 18, 7–43.

Levy, P. (1997) 'A political-economic analysis of free trade agreements', *American Economic Review*, 87(4), 506–19.

Rivera-Batiz, L. (1993) 'Integration among unequals', *Regional Science & Urban Economics*, 23(3), 337–54.

Rugman, A. (1990) *Global Corporate Strategies and Trade Policy*, New York: International Business Series, Routledge.

Scollay, R. and J. Gilbert (2000) 'Measuring the gains from APEC trade liberalization: An overview of CGE assessments', *World Economy*, 23(2), 175–97.

Spilimbergo, A. and Stein, E. (1996) 'The welfare implications of trading blocs among countries with different endowments', NBER Working Paper No. 5472.

Tamura, R. (1995) 'Regional economies and market integration', *Journal of Economic Dynamics and Control*, 20(5), 825–45.

Yamazawa, I. (2001) 'Assessing a Japan–Korea free trade agreement', *Developing Economies*, 39, 3–48.

7
Thailand and New Regionalism

Bhanupong Nidhiprabha

Introduction

The world economy has been increasingly integrated through trade, investment and financial markets over the last three decades. The degree of synchronization of economic activities in the world has become more pronounced. Consequently, developing economies have been adversely affected by fluctuations of the world business cycle. Nevertheless, there is no doubt that high economic growth in developing countries can be attributed to outward-oriented policy which relies on export growth as a driving force. Pro-trade and pro-investment policy has led to continued expansion of industries and increased inflows of foreign direct investment in developing countries. High growth also enables developing countries to successfully reduce their poverty levels.

For Thailand, the process of globalization or closer integration with world commodity markets has been on-going for the last three decades. The share of international trade to GDP also increased tremendously, partly due to the reduction of the government's dependence on international trade taxes. As shown in Figure 7.1, the value of exports and imports has exceeded GDP since 1996. The increasing degree of globalization continues unabated despite the recession of 1998. By 2005, the degree of trade openness had reached 250 per cent of GDP.[1] The size of the international trade sector has doubled the size of GDP, thanks to the economic expansion generated by export growth and importation of capital and intermediate goods for the manufacturing sector. In addition, the fragmentation production processes has led to more trade volume in parts and components of manufactures (Deardorff, 2001).

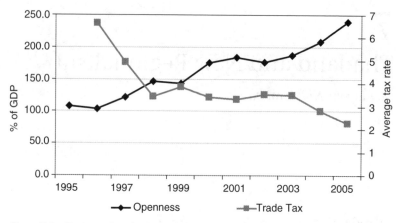

Figure 7.1   Degree of trade openness and average trade tariff

Source: Bank of Thailand and Customs Department.

Thailand's exports of manufactures also responded to tariff reductions in industrial countries through GATT liberalization. According to Abreu (1966), the high tariff wall on manufactures of industrial countries of around 50 per cent in the 1940s was reduced to only 4 per cent by 1988 at the early stage of the Uruguay Round. Similarly between the early 1980s and the late 1990s, the average tariff rates in developing countries were cut in half; by 1999 the average tariff rates of developing countries were only 11 per cent (Martin, 2003). In Thailand, trade reform through the dismantling of tariff walls employed to protect infant industries in the 1960s was undertaken earnestly in the 1980s and continued throughout the 1990s.

The Thai government has relied less on tariff revenue and depended more on revenue collected from direct taxation and value-added taxes. The percentage of international trade tax revenues in total international trade value, a proxy for the tariff rate, had been declining until it became stagnant around 3 per cent between 2000 and 2003 (Figure 7.1). Thailand has reached the stage where it is difficult to further reduce tariff rates, unless further reform is forced by liberalization through commitment imposed by regional trade blocks. Integration into the global economy requires that the tariff rate must fall further. If Thailand cannot do so, it would miss the opportunity to grow, since the structure of world trade has substantially changed from the past decade. Developing countries have shifted from dependence on exports of commodities to relying more on exports of manufactures to developed countries (Martin, 2003). Thailand must open more to take the opportunities to integrate into the rest of the world by allowing free flows of intermediate and capital goods to support the manufacturing sector to compete effectively in the world market.

This chapter addresses prospects and problems of Thailand's attempt to comply with the globalization trend via regional and cross-regional free trade agreements. The remainder of the chapter is divided into five further sections. The next section discusses the nature of Thailand's regional integration. This is followed by an examination of the role of foreign direct investment in Thailand in bringing the country into an integral part of the world markets. Future consequences of public infrastructure investment in the Greater Mekong Sub region are discussed. Section 4 deals with Thailand's attempt simultaneously formulate Free Trade Agreements (FTAs) with countries of various sizes and distances. Motivations, potential benefits, and pitfalls from each proposed FTAs are discussed. Section 5 explores the problems that might arrive from having multiple FTAs. Section 6 provides concluding remarks.

Intensifying regional integration

The share of trading volume intensity between Thailand and ASEAN partners has increased over the years. It demonstrates that Thailand has engaged more in trading with ASEAN countries at the expense of the rest of the world. Thailand previously depended on imports from USA, whose share in total imports of Thailand was 14 per cent in 1980; the share declined to 9.4 per cent in 2003. Import dependence on the EU also declined at a less drastic rate from 13.3 to 10 per cent. The declining import trends from both the EU and US will continue. On the other hand, the share of imports from ASEAN increased gradually from 12 to 16 per cent during the same period. Does it mean that the ASEAN free trade area has created a trade diversion effect? Imports from Japan, China and Korea (JCK) increased more dramatically to 36 per cent in 2002 (Figure 7.2). The currency realignment after 1998 partly explains the shift in Thailand's import structure. Because the baht depreciates against the yen less than the euro and the dollar, imported goods from Japan, Korea and China were relatively cheaper than those goods from USA and the EU, resulting in the rapid rise in Thailand's imports from the Asian region.

As far as Thailand is concerned, FTAs among ASEAN plus three would have a greater impact than FTA between ASEAN and other economic blocks.[2] Consumers and importers of intermediate inputs would benefit considerably from tariff reduction through FTAs among Thailand, Japan and China.

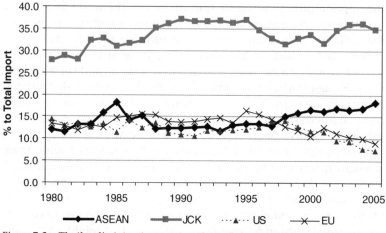

Figure 7.2   Thailand's Asian integration through importation

Source: Bank of Thailand.

In terms of integration through expansion of exports, there has been a considerable increase in exports of Thai products to ASEAN countries, rising from 16 per cent in 1980 to 21 per cent in 2003 (Figure 7.3). When Japan, China, and Korea are included, the corresponding figures rise from 34 to 44 per cent, clearly indicating the benefit that Thailand obtained by gaining access to the three markets. Between 1995 and 1997, the overvaluation of the Thai baht depressed export growth in

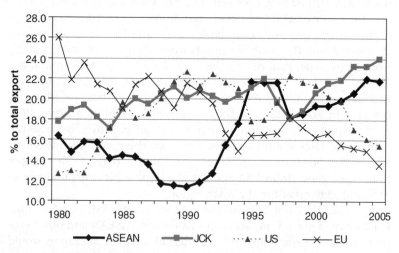

Figure 7.3   Thailand's Asian integration through exportation

Source: Bank of Thailand.

the US market, but the declining trend continued even after the massive baht depreciation. The export share of the ASEAN in totol Thailand's exports has currently surpassed those of the EU and USA. Thailand has more than ever become more and more integrated with her Asian partners.

When analysing import structures of individual ASEAN countries, there is a positive relationship between Thailand's market shares in total imports of ASEAN members and the level of economic development in each country. The old members of ASEAN countries' shares of Thai commodities in their imports are less than 5 per cent, suggesting that Thailand's products do not fit well with their demand patterns. Nevertheless, the Philippines and Indonesia's shares of Thai products increased continuously from 1985 to 2002 (Figure 7.4), while the shares in imports of Singapore and Malaysia exhibit a declining trend since 1995. The two countries have outgrown the specific production structure of Thailand, due to their higher living standards. However, this is not the case for new members of the ASEAN countries. Laos, Cambodia and Myanmar imported more Thai products between 1985 and 2003 as their economy experienced higher income levels. With relatively low transportation cost, the share of Thai goods imported into Laos amounted to 70 per cent in 2004 (Figure 7.5). There would be a great potential for Thai products to gain access to the CLMV countries if the transportation costs and trade barriers can be reduced further. Moreover, as the CLMV countries are growing, their pattern of imports would follow the pattern of the old ASEAN members. The difference

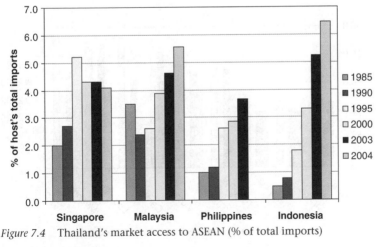

Figure 7.4   Thailand's market access to ASEAN (% of total imports)

Source: UN trade statistics.

would be their closer proximity to Thailand and hence the lower cost of transportation.

If we expand the scope of regional integration to cover all other countries in Asia, ASEAN countries indeed have been trading with other countries in Asia more than ever. This is illustrated in Figures 7.6 and 7.7, which depict cross-sectional data and the snapshots of percentage shares of imports and exports with countries in Asia between 1990 and 2004. The evidence suggests that ASEAN nations increased

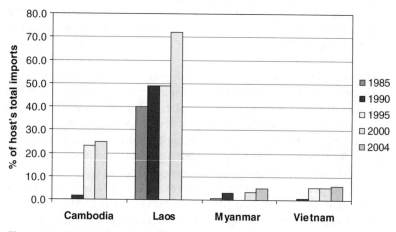

Figure 7.5   Thailand's market access to CLMV (% of total imports)

Source: UN trade statistics.

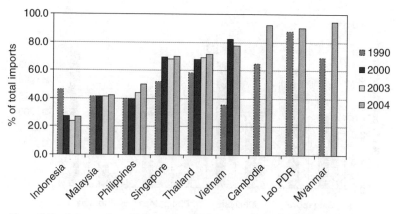

Figure 7.6   Asian regional integration (% of imports from Asia)

Source: WTO.

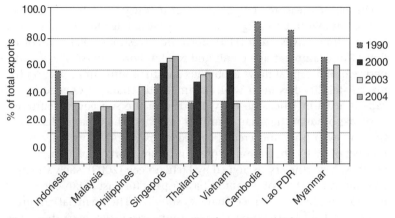

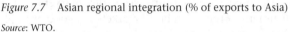

Figure 7.7 Asian regional integration (% of exports to Asia)

Source: WTO.

their trading volumes, both in imports and exports, within Asia as well as within ASEAN countries. The exceptions to the trend are those countries that obtained foreign direct investment in export-oriented industries. Because Cambodia, Indonesia, Lao PDR and Vietnam found their export markets outside Asia, their export to countries in Asia are not large. Furthermore, the comparative advantages of their export products are high relative to the rest of the world, but may be lower than other ASEAN countries.

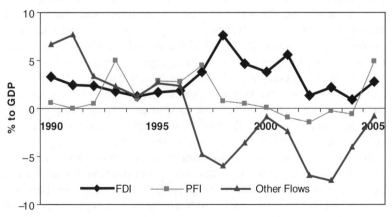

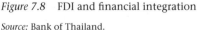

Figure 7.8 FDI and financial integration

Source: Bank of Thailand.

The other measurement of the world integration is the ratio of capital inflows to GDP. Figure 7.8 shows percentage to GDP of the net foreign direct investment (FDI), portfolio investment (PFI), and other flows (for example, trade credit and foreign borrowings). The volatile nature of hot capital flows is obvious and their virulent impact on the macro stability has been well documented. Thailand opened up its capital account since the early 1990s and the subsequent currency crisis has brought the Asian countries together. The Chiang Mai initiative for swap lines and credits agreed to by ASEAN plus three is the product of such cooperation to prevent future shortage of international reserves. Nevertheless, as argued by Eichengreen (2003), such attempts to support a system of common basket pegs for East Asian currencies may not be able to enhance financial stability. The financial resources should instead be devoted to developing securities markets in the region. The establishment of the Asian bond markets is a good example of resource pooling among Asian countries to increase flows of financial resources within Asia.

The role of FDI and infrastructure investment

Foreign direct investment has transformed Thailand's traditional agriculture-based economy into a modern manufacturing economy. Another form of regional integration can be seen from the rising trend of foreign direct investment in the region. Net FDI from ASEAN countries has exceeded those of the US and EU since 2001, while Japan has always been a major investor in Thailand.[3] As pointed out by Kojima (2002), pro-trade-FDI from comparative disadvantage investing countries like Japan that flows to comparative advantage host countries can augment comparative advantage and productivity growth in both home and host countries. The FDI-led growth pattern of a regional economy is a prime motive for building regional integration along the line of the flying-geese model of industrial development. However, as the Japanese economy suffered from a long stagnation, the driving force from the leader of the geese to spur growth for the rest of the flock in Asia has been slowing down, while China also has attracted a substantial share of FDI from the rest of the world.

Since China engaged fully in world trade, the level of FDI in Asian countries has been declining. There was a persistent decline in FDI as a percentage of GDP in Thailand from 1990 to 1996. However there was a surge in FDI that occurred in 1998, amounting to 8 per cent of GDP (Figure 7.8). These increased flows were investment from the EU and

Singapore. They were not in the form of green field investment that flowed in before the Thai banking crisis. They were inflows from capital injection to overtake troubled Thai banks. One might argue that had Thailand opened her banking sector to foreign investors earlier, the cost of financial bailout could have been lowered. However, there is growing opposition to liberalize the service sector because of the fear of competition from more efficient service providers from abroad.

Foreign direct investment that follows trade liberalization can enhance dynamic gains from FTAs. The accumulated stock of foreign direct investment raises the supply capacity of the manufacturing sector; thereby raising the level of exports. The empirical evidence provided by Redding and Venables (2003) shows that more than half of the quadruple increase in Thailand's exports between 1982–85 and 1994–97 stemmed from improvement in internal supply-side conditions. In addition, own-region foreign market access and other-region foreign market access contributed to 43.6 per cent and 17.3 per cent of total export growth, respectively. Export performance is, therefore, strongly related to market access. Differential foreign market access growth can explain the superiority of export performance of South-East Asian nations, when compared to Sub-Saharan Africa, because of ASEAN's higher level of geographical concentration. Regional integration is motivated by close proximity of geographical location.

According to Velde and Morrissey (2004), FDI has raised wage inequality in Thailand because of the consequent impact on increased wages for both skilled and low-skilled workers. Thus FDI could be a source of income inequality within the country. Nevertheless, income inequality depends also on inequality of assets including human capital. The concept of Economic Partnership Agreement (EPA) is very crucial, because it can reduce the cost of adjustment to regionalization. Adverse consequences of FDI across borders must be minimized. Financial assistance toward improving the quality of human capital is needed to accompany increased flows of regional investment.

FDI in the Asian region has been declining as large investments has been diverted into China. Foreign direct investment in the industrial sector of Thailand declined sharply after 2001. There is also an increase in FDI in real estate and service sectors. This is a disturbing trend since that kind of investment would only give more pressure to the appreciation of the real exchange rate. The fact that the proportion of FDI in industry has reduced indicates the decline in capability to export in the future, unless domestic investment can offset the fall.

The decline in FDI can lead to a slowdown in poverty reduction. Mirza and Giroud (2004) produce the evidence that FDI in Thailand has a strong direct effect on poverty reduction through employment generation and consumption multipliers, while its impact on value-chain multipliers and spillovers remain low. The export-oriented manufacturing subsidiaries resulted in little development of forward linkages, while the industries' quality assurance requires high-tech products which must be imported from foreign countries.

To restore the attractiveness of FDI in the region, ASEAN countries need to form a regional economic block to attract Foreign direct investment. Since Japan and Hong Kong are the largest investors in Thailand, the idea of establishing ASEAN plus three or an Asian Economic Community (AEC) provides some hope and lessens the fear of losing FDI to China. But the date set for AEC is the 2020, which is too far in the future. For this reason, Thailand has tried hard to establish FTAs with its major trading partners by breaking away from multilateralism.

Greater Mekong Subregion (GMS) nations, comprising Cambodia, Laos, Myanmar, Thailand, Vietnam and Yunnan province in China, have agreed to promote trade and investment in the region. The Asian Development Bank has agreed to provide loans worth $770 million to finance transportation projects by establishing networks of roads between GMS countries and building bridges across the Mekong River. The East–West Economic Corridor will connect four countries from the port city of Da Nang on the South China Sea in Vietnam to Mawlamyine, a port city on the Andaman Sea in Myanmar, via connecting roads passing through Khon Khan and Phitsanulok in Thailand, and Suvanakhet in Laos. On the North–South Economic Corridor, Chiang Rai province in Northern Thailand can be linked to Kunming in Yunnan via roads passing through Myanmar. On another route on the North–South Economic Corridor, goods can be transported from Kunming to Chiang Rai via Laos. Furthermore, Bangkok can be linked to Phnom Penh and Ho Chi Min City by the Southern Economic Corridor. The infrastructure development in the GMS would develop secondary cities along the road networks and provide access of hinterlands to ports. The planned road networks would connect six countries in the Greater Mekong Region, integrating these countries geographically more than ever.

Transportation cost as well as transaction cost of goods within the subregion can be further reduced by the GMS agreement, effective by 2008, to reduce customs procedures and non-physical barriers for cross border transportation. The role of distance in reducing trade flows has been well established in economic geography literature through gravity trade models (Krugman and Venables, 1995). Economic cost of trade depends on distance and tariff costs. The integration between Thailand and GMS countries would be intensified, because the distances by sea among them are much higher than the planned road network. The expected increase in the trading volume within the GMS region can be thought of as emerging from establishing natural trading blocks, the concept developed by Krugman (1991). The GMS subregional trading bloc is a natural consequence of the reduction in non-tariff trade cost, reinforcing the trade pattern. Lower tariff rates among CLMV countries in the region would not create much trade diversion because their trade volumes with countries outside the bloc are small. On the contrary, trade creation effect would be welfare improving for the subregion.

As pointed out by Venables (2003) globalization can lead to inequality of nations under certain conditions. Integration between low income countries would lead to income divergence, while integration between high income countries can lead to convergence. In the future when all of the economic corridor road networks have been completed, the distance between cites in Thailand and in other CLMV countries can be greatly reduced. When the cost of transportation is reduced, industry may spread out from the centre to periphery countries or clustering of industry may take place in Thailand, because complementary activities to industries are thinly spread in the CLMV countries. As a result, wage rates in CLMV countries may rise or fall relative to the wage rates surrounding the Bangkok areas. If divergence of income occurs, some kinds of economic partnership programmes between GMS areas are required to offset the unintended consequences of regional integration.

Thailand with multiple FTAs

The debacle of the Doha Round of WTO Ministerial meeting in Cancun in September 2003 can be attributed to the objectives in the WTO agenda that go beyond tariff liberalization.[4] The EU pushed the mandate on the so-called 'Singaporean issues', which include regulations on investment, competition policy and government procurement. The EU initiative on compensatory benefits for any concessions on agricultural liberalization was rejected by developing countries led by Brazil, China and India, resulting in the breakdown of the Cancun meeting. As long as the agricultural reform proposed by developed countries was too limited, the successful conclusion of the agreement will be almost impossible.

Because of the WTO deadlock, there has been growing attempts by countries in Asia to forge ahead with alternative free trade agreements. Dent (2003) argued that the proliferation of Asia-Pacific bilateral free trade agreements represents the failures of APEC, the WTO and the AFTA of ASEAN.[5] The new bilateral trend has departed significantly from diffuse reciprocity principle, upon which WTO multilateralism and APEC's open regionalism are based. The new trend is based on a specific reciprocity basis on which the free trade agreements are negotiated. Desker (2004) argued that multilateral agreement at the WTO, though optimal, is not practical. Asian countries should adopt the bilateral and regional FTA negotiations which are more pragmatic in the short run, while they can pursue global trade negotiations in the long run.

Thailand's rush to negotiate FTAs with many countries, including Chile and Peru, can be attributed to a reaction to other countries' attempts to formulate free trade agreements with Thailand's major trading countries like Japan and the US. Thai negotiators are well aware of the 'spaghetti bowl' effect, as dubbed by Bhagwati *et al.* (1998), where firms have difficulties comprehending a wide range of different foreign trading arrangements caused by overlapping bilateral FTAs. It should be noted the fear of the spaghetti bowl effect may be over stressed. Small and medium size firms would not be able to diversify their export markets to the extent that they are 'confused' by specific requirements in the FTAs. Large firms with higher degree of export diversification would be rational and capable enough to exploit selective markets that yield maximum profits made available to them through multiple FTAs.

Thailand does not want to be too late, as FDI might be lured away into countries that have established FTAs with the US and Japan. In addition, Thailand's export competitiveness can be eroded due to the tariff concession given to countries that form FTAs with Thailand's major trading partners. Multiple FTAs are a new logical trade strategy for Thailand.

FTAs are only part of the New Economic Partnership (NEP), which includes cooperation in other areas, including financial assistance to alleviate the burden of adjustment costs. This is also a strong argument for having FTAs with large countries such as Japan, USA and China. According to Urata and Kiyota (2003), Thailand would gain most from establishing FTAs with East Asian nations because of existing high tariff barriers.

Table 7.1   Thailand's free trade agreements status

Country	Under feasibility study	Process of negotiation	Early implementation	Date of implementation	Year to complete FTA framework agreement
		Status of FTA			
Bahrain		x	x	Dec-02	n.a.
ASEAN-China		x	x	Oct-03	2015
India		x	x	Oct-03	2010
Australia		x	x	Jan-05	2025
New Zealand		x	x	Jul-05	2015
Peru		x	x	Nov-05	2015
BIMSTEC*		x	x	Jul-06	Fast track by 2011 and Normal track by 2017
Japan		x			
USA		x			
EPTA		x			
Mexico	x				
ASEAN-Korea	x				
Thailand–China	x				

* Economic cooperation between Bangladesh, Bhutan, India, Myanmar, Nepal, Sri Lanka and Thailand.

Source: Ministry of Commerce.

It is always easier to negotiate between the two parties if they have fewer conflicts and issues to resolve, especially if they are small, although the gains would not be large. Bahrain was the first country with which Thailand concluded a FTA (Table 7.1). Although the volume of trade between the two countries is less than $150 million annually, it is the first FTA that Thailand has ever formulated. Thailand has been in the process of learning by negotiating with Bahrain, a small country which exports fertilizer, oil and aluminum to Thailand. Those imported products were subject to an average 20 per cent tariff rate. As a result of the conclusion of the negotiations, the agreed tariff rate was reduced to 3 per cent, which is even lower than the rate Thailand imposes on ASEAN countries at 5 per cent. The FTA with Bahrain, though not comprehensive, is important since it implies that FTAs can actually reduce, instead of increasing, the trade diversion effect since the tariff rate imposed on the new FTA partners is lower than the one imposed on member ASEAN countries. The FTA with Australia is the most comprehensive agreement because of the inclusion of the service sector. Thai investors can hold 100 per cent of equity in all sectors except those related to security. On the commodity side, tariff reductions came into effect in January 2005. The Australian government has reduced the tariff rates on 80 per cent of the import items to zero. Textile and automobile sectors in Thailand will benefit from the agreement. In 2003, imports of textiles from Thailand were less than 1 per cent of Australia's total textile imports. Hence, there would be more room for Thailand's textile industry, which suffered from the end of the 40 years of import quota system up to January 2005. The low-cost textile and clothing industries in China and India would gain market shares in the US at the expense of other developing countries including Thailand and Cambodia.[6] The FTAs with Australia would immediately cut the existing tariff rate of 25 per cent to 12.5 per cent, bringing in the cost advantage of Thai products over China, Indonesia and India whose products are subject to the 25 per cent tariff rate. Furthermore, the local content is set at 30 per cent, while 25 per cent of raw materials can come from other developing countries.

Thailand pick-up trucks and Australia's large cars are complementary in the automobile markets of both countries. Intra-industry trade in the automotive sectors can enhance the efficiency of the industries in both countries due to the FTA-enhanced opportunity to exploit economies of scale through expansion of sales between the two countries. While imports of Japanese pick-up trucks amount to 41 per cent of the Australian market, Thai pick-up trucks and small cars account for 38 per cent, and 2 per cent respectively. It is expected that sales of Thai pick-up trucks and passenger cars after 2005 would increase considerably.

Some inefficient and small farm sectors in Thailand would not be able to compete with cheap Australian products. However, Thailand has been importing more than the minimum requirement of 55,000 tons of milk, as committed by Thailand at the Uruguay Round. Furthermore, Thailand barely charges any tariffs on milk. Thus the fear of adverse impact of FTAs on the Thai milk industry is exaggerated. Nevertheless, non-tariff barriers such as sanitary and phytosanitary conditions must be agreed upon to make sure that they are not substitutes for the tariff reductions. As it turns out, Thailand has been slower than Australia in the reduction of the tariff rates. Some of Thailand's manufacturing sector could take the full benefit of importing metal such as iron ore, copper and zinc from Australia.

The Thai–Australia FTAs are employed as a model for establishing FTAs between Thailand and New Zealand. Both agreements are comprehensive. Nevertheless, the timeframe for cutting the tariff on dairy products was suggested by New Zealand to be shortened below the 20 years' timeframe agreed in the Australia–Thai FTAs. Thailand has already imported butter and cheese from New Zealand, but the high transportation costs prohibit imports of fresh milk.

The Thai–New Zealand FTAs can serve as a model for the creation of the regional trade pact between ASEAN and the Closer Economic Co-operation (CEC) countries of Australia and New Zealand. The Thailand–China FTA can be served as a basis for an ASEAN–China FTAs. According to the statistics obtained from almost 14,000 rules of origin certificates issued by Customs Department, one year after the introduction of the fast track FTAs with China, exports of Thai fruits and vegetables increased to almost 14 billion baht. The Thai tapioca industry also benefited because of the strong demand from China to manufacture alcohol and acid. Tapioca exports to China increased by more than 35 per cent in 2004.[7]

While Thailand can substantially increase her exports of tropical fruits like durian, longan, mango and mangosteen to China, imports of Chinese pears and grapes also increase tremendously. The demand for imported Chinese vegetables such as garlic, carrots, onions and potatoes is price elastic. The volume of imports increased dramatically as a result of the tariff cut. Consumers in both countries have enjoyed the benefit in terms of cost and varieties. There is no doubt that FTAs can reduce the inflationary pressure of agriculture products during off seasons and drought. Thai farmers cannot compete with Chinese farmers producing garlic and onions; their costs of production are as low as 40 per cent of the farm-gate prices in Thailand. Resistance to these adjustments through subsidies or guaranteed prices would only prolong the problem of inefficiency. There is no need for intervention by the government, because Thai farmers would be able to adjust in the long run by responding to a new price structure established by the FTAs to reallocate resources to more efficient production. It should be noted that China–ASEAN FTAs would be completed by 2010. An early harvest programme with China and Thailand would serve as a stepping stone toward a wider regionalism.

FTAs between Thailand and India are similar to China's due to the initiation of the fast track deal. Tariff reduction on 82 products is covered under the fast track programme that came into effect in September 2004. The two countries have larger population but lower average income than Thailand. In this sense, Thailand would not be at disadvantage as many Thai products are complementary to those in India and China. Both China and India are growing rapidly for different reasons. China is growing fast by the heavy foreign direct investment and public infrastructure investment, while India is growing rapidly because of the enlarging private sector. Three hundred million Indian consumers would become very attractive to Thai investors, after Thai exports have made their impact in the Indian markets of electronic products, machinery and jewellery. At the same time, Thai jewellery industry would benefit from imported gems as cheap inputs to their industry. Viewed in this light, Thailand has made an important selection of FTA partners that are full of dynamism and great potential.

The other benefit from establishing a FTA with India is that it is a foundation for strengthening the regional grouping of the BIMST–EC (Table 7.1) between the two ASEAN (Thailand and Burma) and the five South Asian countries of India, Bangladesh, Bhutan, Nepal and Sri Lanka). The group has a plan to negotiate free-trade agreements for goods, investment and services and cooperation in the field of technology, communications, energy, and tourism. In the long run, BIMST–EC can serve as a bridge between ASEAN and the South Asian Association for Regional Cooperation (SAARC). Again, these kinds of bilateral FTAs initiations do not totally depart from the spirit of regional integration and multilateralism; they strengthen the foundation for future regional integration.

Under WTO agreements, contingency measures are authorized in the forms of safeguards, countervailing duties and anti-dumping duties (ADD). Because Thailand's exports to the world market are growing rapidly, they are subject to targets of ADD by importing countries. According to empirical evidence provided by Head and Ries (2004), between 1995 and 2002, Thailand had been targeted by importing countries with ADD more proportionately than her share of world's exports, but Japan seldom uses ADD although her share in world's imports is more than 5 per cent. However, boneless chicken has been a trade dispute between Thailand and Japan for many years. Other sensitive products that Japan feels uncomfortable with during FTA negotiations are rice, sugar and tapioca. Thailand's sensitive commodities include hot-rolled steel sheets.

The benefits that Thailand would receive from the free trade negotiation with Japan are probably the greatest among all FTA deals. For Thailand, Japan is the largest trading partner and the biggest source of foreign direct investment. There are more than one million Japanese visitors to Thailand each year. The negotiations extend beyond free trade agreements. The so-called Economic Partnership Agreement (EPA) includes cooperation in education, environment, energy, sciences and technology, tourism and human resource development. Note that EPA goes beyond what WTO has stipulated since it allows partners to take advantage of each other's strength and recognize the value of cooperation.

Although Japan has already established FTAs with Singapore, Thailand is a more difficult case for Japan, since negotiations involve agriculture and labour issues. Singapore had already removed most of her tariff barriers, while the two countries' levels of per capita income do not differ much. The success of the FTA negotiation is so important that Thailand had to withdraw rice from the negotiation.[8] Obviously the outcome of the negotiations depends on the bargaining power of each party. But international politics are also important as China is exerting its power in economic cooperation with ASEAN countries. Thailand would like to have large countries such as China, India and the US involved to reduce the dominant power of a single large economy. Withdrawing rice and hot-rolled steel sheets from trade liberalization would make negotiations in other sectors possible if rice is as important for Japan as much as hot-rolled steel sheets for Thailand. Furthermore, Thailand would have gained much more than having struck no deal at all. Rice is not the only agricultural product that Thailand has comparative advantage in the world markets, but there must be a limit to such compromise. The exclusion list cannot go on until most protectionists are happy about the deal.

As pointed out by Naya (2004), FTAs are crucial for structural adjustments of Japan in order to maintain her global competitiveness and remain a leader in the world economy. FTAs with Thailand and other ASEAN countries can provide Japan an opportunity to grow closer to other Asian countries, while collectively protecting themselves from negative effects of regional agreements in Europe and Northern America. The successful conclusion of the FTAs between Thailand and Japan would benefit the two countries more if they do not hold on to the protection of comparative disadvantage sectors. Bhagwati (2004) argued that most bilateral trade agreements exempt agriculture and few exist between countries with competing farm sectors. Perhaps the FTAs between Thailand and Japan can be an example of the FTAs that include agricultural sectors – albeit without rice. Because the US is the largest export destination for Thailand, FTA negotiation with the US might be the most difficult. The issue of intellectual property rights covering software and pharmaceutical industries, has become an obstacle to reaching the deal. It is understandable that extending the longevity of patents can maintain the monopoly power of American companies as they would gain more incentives for their research and innovation. But the high prices of these products would also reduce the utilization of products that are crucial for healthcare and the development of the software industry in Thailand. Thai negotiators call for a lifting of compulsory license for retroviral drugs to combat HIV or for vaccines against SARS and avian flu as permitted by the WTO.[9] There are many points to be negotiated before the conclusion of the deal. There are also much more to trade off between the two nations in order to strike a deal if they really want to come up with any fruitful FTAs. Some parties that gain substantially from the deals should be able to compensate those parties that lose considerably after the conclusion of the negotiations.

Tables 7.3 and 7.4 provide percentage changes in trade volume between Thailand and other countries with which Thailand attempts to establish free trade agreements. Although the complete agreements

Table 7.2   Thailand's exports to potential FTA countries (percentage change)

Export destination	2004	2005
Bahrain	27.4	28.9
China	25.1	29.1
India	43.1	67.7
Australia	14.3	28.9
New Zealand	24.2	58.2
Peru	64.9	41.3
BIMSTEC	37.8	35.1
Japan	18.9	12.3
USA	14.1	10.0
EPTA	–16.1	–3.6
Mexico	12.3	1.6
Korea	17.4	21.6

Source: Ministry of Commerce, Bank of Thailand.

Table 7.3 Thailand's imports from FTA countries (percentage change)

Sources of imports	2004	2005
Bahrain	–7.0	35.9
China	35.7	37.0
India	30.5	12.4
Australia	42.2	48.0
New Zealand	13.0	6.8
Peru	14.9	6.7
BIMSTEC	38.5	23.9
Japan	23.3	16.9
USA	1.6	20.5
EPTA	18.5	49.3
Mexico	–6.6	25.3
Korea	23.8	8.4

Source: Ministry of Commerce, Bank of Thailand.

have yet to materialize in the future (Table 7.1), Thailand's trade deficits with China and Australia increased as imports rose faster than exports in 2004 and 2005. One of the critiques of Thailand's free trade agreements is based on the FTA impact on worsening trade balances. It should be noted that trade balances between countries are a bad indicator of well-being of a nation, because they do not reflect efficient allocation of resources in production and consumption. Furthermore, there are other factors, such as exchange rates and economic growth, affecting trade flows between countries.

The way forward

Although the new trading strategy of Thailand seems appropriate, success depends on how the plans are executed in detail. Because FTAs always involve losers and gainers, unreasonable fear of changes, frictions and adjustment costs are high in the short run. FTAs always include rules of origin. There are employed to prevent an exporter from exploiting a low tariff 'backdoor' by introducing products that would have been subject to high tariffs since they are not produced in the member countries of the regional trading bloc. These rules, if they are not standardized when Thailand has completed FTAs with various countries, can create high administrative and transaction costs, stifling the intended effect of trade creation. Those rules of origin must be simplified to facilitate administration procedure without causing trade diversion or act as a hidden instrument to protect domestic industry. It should be noted that if Thailand continues to reduce MFN tariff rates, the cost associated with the rules of origin can also be reduced. The upper boundary of those costs is the MFN tariff rate, because it would not be worthwhile for firms if the compliance cost to the rules of origin is greater than the benefit derived from a particular tariff treatment offered by the FTAs.

With the recent trend of increasing degree of trade fragmentation, trade occurs more frequently between nations in the region to obtain parts and components of manufactures. Rules of origin can be manipulated to suppress trade when it diverts trade from efficient producers abroad to high cost intermediate products of domestic industry. It is more likely in the case of manufactures than agriculture since each manufactured product has its own specific nature and production standard. The hidden technical details of the rules of origin can be manipulated to suit protectionists' interests. Thus rules of origin can create trade deflection if they lead to the import of intermediate products from inefficient producers of the FTA partners with the lowest external tariff.

In the case of Thailand, automobiles, textiles and electronics are important manufacturing sectors both in terms of output and employment. These industries might be affected by rules of origin if Thailand does not have enough bargaining power against large economies to establish a series of identical rules of origin among them. To prevent multiple series of FTAs from creating the so-called 'hub and spoke' pattern within the ASEAN region, diagonal cumulation of the rules of origin is needed.[10] Thus exports of textiles from Thailand to Australia can be subject to 30 per cent of local content required by the rules of origin and the Thai textile industry can employ up to 30 per cent of intermediate inputs from another ASEAN country if that particular ASEAN country has already establised FTAs with Australia. Moving to a system of diagonal cumulation of rules of origin widens possible sources of intermediate suppliers to countries which are part of the system, resulting in trade creation and trade reorientation (Augier *et al.* 2004). In that sense, other ASEAN's FTAs negotiations with the countries that Thailand has already concluded negotiations must be encouraged to enhance the intra-industry trade in the region.

Although the WTO permits importing countries to impose regulations on environment, food safety, animal welfare and hygienic standards, negotiations must be carried out to remove arbitrary regulations on such issues. The arbitrary nature of rules and regulations is more serious impediments to trade than tariff rates, because they impose cost as well as risk and uncertainty. Negotiations regarding the non-tariff barriers, safeguard clauses, and Sanitary and Phytosanitary Standard (SPS) must be included in the FTAs deal.

The dynamic impact of the new regional integration would result in differential growth rates of member countries. As argued by Venables (2003), convergence of income depends on relative comparative advantage of the country relative to the rest of the world. The FTAs that Thailand has planned to establish with Japan and the US, therefore, are likely to give net benefit to Thailand. It is highly beneficial for Thailand to engage in establishing FTAs with higher income countries – the 'North–South' agreements – because their economic activities are complementary. However, the exclusion list of sensitive commodities should be kept at a minimum on both sides.

Some of the FTAs that Thailand has made are not comprehensive. The Thai government must negotiate continuously to expand product coverage. The successful results of the fast track agreement would enable the public to reap the benefit of free trade and accept the fact that those comparative disadvantage sectors must adjust themselves to the force of globalization.

Concluding remarks

Thailand has increasingly become an integral part of the world economy, but the degree of regional integration of Thailand has been more pronounced in Asia. There is an important realization after the 1998 currency crisis that countries in Asia must cooperate in terms of economic policy. The Chiang Mai initiative in May 2000 aims to prevent currency attacks and crisis contagion in the future. Through arrangements made by central banks in the region, countries in trouble must be provided with $40 billion during the period of liquidity shortage. Moreover, the Asian Bond markets are also a product of the Asia Cooperation Dialogue (ACD), aiming at promoting capital markets in the region to lessen heavy dependence on financial resources from other parts of the world.

The tariff rates among ASEAN countries have been cut to 5 per cent, covering about 95 per cent of intra-ASEAN trade. Furthermore, the time frame is set at the year 2010 for fully liberalized trade among the ASEAN Six, and the new members by 2015. The deadline has been set at 2020 for the establishment of an Asian Economic Community (AEC). However, that dateline might be too far for Asian countries to remain competitive in an era of intensified regional groupings. It is possible that investment diversion from Asia can be more overwhelming than the trade diversion impact of other regional groupings. To forge ahead, FTAs are the only choice consistent with the framework of regional integration.

Having multiple FTAs with developed and developing countries would ensure Thailand would obtain benefits from having free trade with many countries in the world at the same time, rather than having to wait forever for the conclusion of the WTO multilateralism. Will more spokes added to the hub lead to the more diluted benefits for each of the spokes? On the contrary, as long as newly established FTAs have more or less similar rules of origin, we can reduce, if it exists, the *spaghetti bowl* effect. After all, the total trade volume between Thailand and negotiated FTAs members (including ASEAN) would amount to more than 60 per cent of Thailand's total trade. Though discriminatory in nature, FTAs proponents have asked the right question: why forsake the opportunity to grow and why wait for the elusive outcome of the multilateral negotiations? FTA supporters are a free trader in a hurry.

Because trade creation and diversion effects depend on price elasticities, the net welfare effect of regional FTAs would depend on whether cross-price elasticities between members and non-members are greater than the price elasticity between products produced within the trading blocs. If Thailand successfully negotiates FTAs with Japan, China and the US, the trade diversion impact would be small, because the three countries' shares in Thailand's trade are substantial. Within the ASEAN countries, the changing comparative advantage would dictate the direction of intra-regional trade pattern. CLMV countries would import more from Thailand, which in turn import more from Singapore and higher income countries in the region. Since manufactured goods produced in high income countries are close substitutes for their imports from low income countries, the impact of regional integration would ensure a considerable welfare gain through trade creation for both importing and exporting countries. At the same time, if these partners in the regional free trade agreement are committed to trade reform, the impact of trade diversion would be minimal as their MFN would continue to decline over time.

But there are some trade-offs and some adverse consequences of the new regionalism. As long as the net benefits of expansion along the line of globalization exist, we should cautiously go ahead with multiple FTAs. We should not let short-term minor adverse impacts obscure the long-term macro dynamic gains from rapid integration into the world economy. Integrating the Thai economy with regional trade blocks can serve as an instrument to speed up domestic reform. Without firm datelines imposed by FTAs, there would be less enthusiastic efforts to carry out difficult reform as the financial crisis might seem to be just a short episode in the Thai economic history. As pointed out by Ethier (1998), an important motivation for countries to sign up for multilateral trade agreements is to help realize economic reform at home, but they are less effective in comparison with preferential trade agreements. Therefore, there is a positive relationship between preferential, regional, and multilateral paths to trade liberalization. The substantial progress at the multilateral level has made FTAs more attractive.

The comparative disadvantage sectors would strongly protest against FTAs, fearing that they would not be able to compete and would soon be wiped out. Political economy will play an important part in deciding the direction of the FTAs. Political will is a crucial factor in determining the speed and the coverage of the regional integration. In addition, economic growth and macroeconomic stability would enable Thailand to forge ahead with regional integration, which must be in line with the goal of multilateralism. The surge in the number of Thailand's FTA negotiations should not be interpreted as diminished commitment to multilateralism. However, the collapse of the Doha round of trade talks in 2006 bodes well for the unrealistic view of multilateralism, trying to avoid hub-and-spoke, and the spaghetti bowl effect of multiple FTAs.

Notes

1. City states such as Hong Kong and Singapore have a higher degree of openness, amounting to 250 and 280 per cent of GDP in 2002. Among other counties in the ASEAN, only Malaysia has a higher level of trade openness around 196 per cent. Small countries tend to have higher degree of trade openness due to their small shares of output in the world markets, while large countries tend to appear insular because of their relative sheer sizes.
2. For an excellent account of the evolution of Asian integration from the formation of APEC to ASEAN plus 3, see Naya (2004).

3. The shares of FDI from Japan, ASEAN and Hong Kong were 43, 36 and 18 per cent respectively in 2003. Other top five investors are USA and the EU, but their relative importance has been declining since the early 2000s.

4. For an optimistic view on the multilateralism, see Bhagwati (2004), who argued that as long as the G-22 and the Cairns Group want agriculture to liberalize, they can only succeed in the context of multilateral agreement. Cancun will serve as a stepping stone to a successful conclusion of the Doha Round of trade negotiation. The Tokyo Round took more than 5 years to finalize, while the Uruguay Round took more than 7 years to complete. Thus the delay of the Doha Round cannot be considered as a failure.

5. According to Dent (2003), Asian Pacific bilateral trade agreements rose from nine participating states with 13 projects by the end of 1999 to 39 projects and 13 perpetrating states by mid 2002.

6. WTO predicted that the market shares of imported clothes to the US from China would increase from 16 to 50 per cent, India from 4 to 15 per cent in the post-quota era.

7. Thailand's major export markets for tapioca are European Union, South Korea, and Japan.

8. The Japanese negotiators would like Thailand to withdraw chickens from the negotiation in exchange for the ratification of the sanitary standard of the Thai chicken industry. This request is unreasonable considering the fact that the share of Thailand's chicken exports amounted to 40 per cent of Japan's total imports, despite the 1.9 per cent import duties.

9. The United Nations World Intellectual Property Organization (WIPO) has adopted a development agenda to consider different intellectual property systems that are appropriate to particular developing countries, which are in dire need for open-source software and drugs for human resource development for the poor.

10. According to Augier *et al.* (2004), rules of origin imposed within the Southern Mediterranean partner countries led to both trade suppression and trade diversion. The lack of cumulation of the rules of origin may restrict trade between non-cumulating countries by up to 80 per cent.

References

Abreu, M. (1966) 'Trade in manufactures: The outcome of the Uruguay Round and developing country interest', in W. Martin and L. A. Winters (eds), *The Uruguay Round and the Developing Countries*, Cambridge: Cambridge University Press.

Augier, P., M. Gasiorek and C. Lai-tong (2004) 'Rules of origin and the EU-Med Partnership: The case of textiles', *The World Economy*, 27(9), 1449–74.

Bhagwati, J. (2004) 'Don't cry for Cancun', *Foreign Affairs*, January/February, 52–63.

Bhagwati, J., D. Greenaway and A. Panagariya (1998) 'Trading preferentially: Theory and policy', *Economic Journal*, 108 (July), 1128–48.

Deardorff, A. (2001) 'International provision of trade services, trade, and fragmentation', *Review of International Economics*, 9(2), 233–48.

Dent, C. M. (2003) 'Networking the region? The emergence and impact of Asia-Pacific bilateral free trade agreement projects', *The Pacific Review*, 16(1), 1–28.

Desker, B. (2004) 'In defense of FTAs: From purity to pragmatism in East Asia', *The Pacific Review*, 17(1), 2–26.

Eichengreen, B. (2003) 'What to do with the Chiang Mai initiative', *Asian Economic Papers*, 2(1), 1–52.

Ethier, W. J. (1998) 'The new regionalism', *Economic Journal*, 108 (July), 1149–61.

Fujita, M., P. Krugman and A. J. Venables (1999) *The Spatial Economy: Cities, Regions, and International Trade*, Boston, MA: MIT Press.

Head, K. and J. Ries (2004) 'Regionalism within multilateralism: The WTO review of Canada', *The World Economy*, 27(9), 1377–400.

Kojima, K. (2002) 'Asian economic integration for the 21st century', *East Asian Economic Perspectives*, March, 1–38.

Krugman, P. (1991) *The Move to Free Trade Zone. Policy Implications of Trade and Currency Zones*, Federal Reserve Bank of Kansas City.

Krugman, P. and A. J. Venables (1995) 'Globalization and the inequality of nations', *Quarterly Journal of Economics*, 110, 857–80.

Martin, W. (2003) 'Developing countries' changing participation in world trade', *The World Bank Research Observer*, 18(2), 187–203.

Mirza, H. and A. Giroud (2004) 'Regionalization, foreign direct investment and poverty reduction', *Journal of the Asia Pacific Economy*, 9(2), 223–48.

Naya, S. F. (2004) 'Japan in emerging East Asian Regionalism', *East Asian Economic Perspectives*, 15(2), 1–16.

Redding, S. and A. J. Venables (2003) 'South-East Asian export performance: External market access and internal supply capacity', *Japanese and International Economics*, 17(4), December, 404–31.

Urata, S. and K. Kiyota (2003) 'The impacts of an East Asia FTA on foreign trade in East Asia', NBER Working Paper No. 10173.

Velde, D. T. and O. Morrissey (2004) 'Foreign direct investment, skills and wage inequality in East Asia', *Journal of the Asia Pacific Economy*, 9(3), 348–69.

Venables, A. J. (2003) 'Winners and losers from regional integration agreements', *The Economic Journal*, 113(490), October, 747–61.

8
Summary of the Panel Discussion

Edited by Masahisa Fujita

This chapter presents the summary of the panel discussion which took place following the presentation of the three papers on the prospects and tasks of regional integration in East Asia (note: the revised versions of the three papers are contained respectively in Chapters 5 to 7).

In addition to Dr Yu Yongding (China), Dr Young Han Kim (South Korea) and Dr Bhanupong Nidhiprabha (Thailand), Dr Paul Krugman and Dr Anthony J. Venables participated in the Panel Discussion, while Masahisa Fujita served as the moderator.

Dr Masahisa Fujita, President, IDE-JETRO

First I would like to ask Dr Paul Krugman about his reaction to the three presentations, namely China, Korea and Thailand, and also wider issues he would like to address. I also would like to have some dialogue with Dr Venables about his presentation and other presentations from these three Asian countries.

Dr Paul R. Krugman, Professor of Economics and International Affairs, Princeton University

I would like to raise two points – the first point is very much following on Dr Yu's presentation. One of the really dramatic conclusions is that East Asia as an integrated economic system already exists and China is the assembly point of this system, looking at the data that we have covered and discussed. Although this may be an oversimplification, you have shipped intermediate goods, or components, to China and then assembled in China and exported back to other East Asian countries and the rest of the world. What that means is that we have a very misleading number or a very misleading perception of the world, if you just look at the direct trade data. The very large Chinese trade

162

surplus with the United States, now US$120 or US$130 billion annual, is not really a Chinese trade surplus. It is really an Asian trade surplus with the United States. China is the assembly point, or the final stop in this integrated East Asian production system. Actually Japan has been, in a diplomatic sense, a beneficiary of this system. By the numbers, it appears that the bilateral Japanese surplus with the United States has dwindled in relative importance, but actually it is just being laundered through China. So in some sense, it is really just a continuing Asian surplus.

I would agree with Dr Yu that this system is not sustainable; although I am not sure we have quite the same view about the lack of sustainability. I would say there are two issues. One is political. It is really difficult to be sure how serious that is, but certainly whenever the United States job market is weak, we have a lot of protectionist rhetoric. It certainly is reflected in pressure, particularly currency policy pressure on China. The other point is simply the unsustainability of the general current account imbalances. The United States has external deficits of more than 5 per cent of gross domestic product (GDP), rapidly building up of external liabilities, and those liabilities takes the form of debt almost entirely, primarily debt to Asian central banks. Something is going to give here. We will talk about which part of Asia is going to decide to try to get out of dollars before the whole thing collapses, precipitating the collapse.

On both the papers by Dr Kim and Dr Nidhiprabha, there are some issues here involving the prospects for East Asian trade integration.

The first thing to say is that the data show how large the trade flows within East Asia are, considering that it is not that compact an area. Although North America is a large area, in terms particularly of United States/Canadian trade, the distances are relatively short by Asian standards. By European standards, this East Asian area is physically enormous; yet the Asian intra-regional trade is larger than North America now, and it is not too far short of intra-European trade, despite the absence of a formal trade agreement, or East Asian free trade area.

So why should that be the case? I think the answer comes back to the end of Dr Fujita's talk: the diversity. Although the political economy of integration is easier for a region of very similar nations, the potential gains from trade are larger when the nations are very different. The fact that you have these very large differences in technology, in per capita income, and in resources among the Asian countries, gives rise to a large amount of trade than you have in the other major economic blocks in the world, despite the existence of larger distances, larger geographic barriers. We have this rise of a very important, very powerful trading block, which is, from an economic point of view, driven by the diversity of the region. The reasons the market can drive it is that there is so much diversity and, therefore, so much comparative advantage within Asia.

However the same diversity creates difficulties for pushing integration further. The deep integration that the Europeans have sought, or the deep integration that actually exists within the United States is possible because you have a great deal of political homogeneity, which is not something that can easily be achieved in Asia. The words 'fiscal federalism' have occurred repeatedly in our discussions here. Fiscal federalism is easy to do if you have a relatively homogeneous area in terms of per capita income because then you can establish some broad compensatory schemes that do not amount to a systematically persistent resource transfer. The United States can have a unified system of social insurance. If there is some resource transfer – some parts of the United States persistently transfer resources to other parts, but those are relatively small shares of GDP. If you try to establish a common social insurance system even within Europe, there would be very large transfers from the wealthier to the poorer regions, and within Asia it would be unthinkable. So the diversity now creates an obstacle to deep integration.

Dr Venables did not stress this quite as much as I would, but it was there: the European story about the politically driven integration. Very much that is a matter of shared political goals, shared political values. If you actually look at the success of enlargements of the European Union (EU) at each point, in effect, the core countries have treated admission into the EU as a reward for democratization. The first big enlargement, the southern European enlargement, was basically, 'Okay, you got rid of your dictators; now you can join.' The second wave now taking place is basically, 'Okay, you got rid of communism; now you can join.' It is very difficult to see anything comparable in Asia, given the political diversity of the region.

There may be a way forward here, but the Asian story is going to be very different. Asia as an economic block does now start to look co-equal with the EU and North America; but it is going to be very, very different from the other two in terms of the actual structure of the relationship.

Dr Anthony J. Venables, Professor of International Economics, London School of Economics and Political Science

I would like to organize my comments by going back to fundamentals in the way we think about regional integration schemes, the costs and benefits of such schemes. I guess all arguments ultimately come down to three forces: trade creation, trade diversion and terms of trade effects.

Trade creation: There are big opportunities for trade creation in Asia, partly because of its diversity and partly because of the production networks, the complementarities in the production structure. So I think that possibilities for trade creation are big.

But there are a couple of other comments on trade creation. The presentation on Korea suggested that Korean objectives should be about minimizing the impact on production. But the theory of comparative advantage suggests almost the opposite; it should be about maximizing the impact on production. It is by having things changed that you get the gains from trade. Similarly it is suggested that Korea is worried about being squeezed between higher technology and lower wage countries, and that seems too dichotomous to me. There is a continuum of industries, there are thousands of activities. You could have clusters in high tech or medium tech or low tech. The idea that middle income countries get squeezed says that rich countries should have free trade, low income countries should have free trade, but middle income ones should do something else. I don't think this argument is reasonable. There are potentially large gains from trade creation with adjustment costs, but those costs have to be confronted.

Trade diversion: I think this must be the first conference I have been to on regional integration where the word 'trade diversion' basically has not been mentioned. Trade diversion is a cost; it brings losses to countries as preferential trade agreements mean that you are not sourcing your imports from the cheapest source. Trade diversion happens out there in the world. Losses are possible. It worries me a bit thinking of what we have heard about the Thailand's case. If there really is a sort of Thai–Peru agreement, is that really a viable trade creation, or is there just a little bit of diversion going on? It is hard to believe that Peru is the lowest-cost source of supply for anything to Thailand or visa versa. I may be wrong. Okay anchovies, thank you. But nevertheless, trade diversion needs to be thought through.

Terms of trade effects: The third mechanism is of real income gains or losses in terms of trade effects. You can change the price of your exports and the price of your imports. Suppose you had a lot of hub and spoke agreements and you were the hub, then that gives you good market access to a lot of places, and that will raise your wages, and that is the terms of trade improvement for you. But the problem with terms of trade improvements is that it is a zero sum gain; one country's terms of trade improvement are another's terms of trade loss. Or to put it differently, not everyone can be a hub; only one country can be a hub in a particular area. That is a zero sum game to do with terms of trade, or probably a negative sum gain actually because it is a bad way of organizing your trade.

Other more or less random comments: the domino logic. I get the sense there is a bit of a rush now for everyone to be in an integration scheme. Yes, there certainly is a domino logic; you do not want to be left out. But what are the benefits of being the first in? What are the costs of being last in? Does it matter? I suppose I can think of two costs of being last in; one is that other people set the rules, and that does matter a bit. Certainly Britain complains about the EU because it never bothered to show up at the stages when the rules were being made. The second point comes out of the logic of geography, clusters. You are going to lose out on a cluster getting set up somewhere else. But doing a sort of reality check on it, I am not sure. Certainly if we look at the EU, Ireland has got the software cluster and Finland has done fine on high tech, and they are both late entrants. I guess the point is that there is quite a lot of fluidity, quite a lot of change in the world with new technologies, certainly in Asia. In these countries, you are not going to be locked into clusters or out of clusters in perpetuity. There is a lot of fluidity going on, so the cost of being last in is not clear.

One final comment just related to something I said earlier: I said that cash is sometimes a way to lubricate deals. I really did not mean that to be interpreted as you should compensate every possible loser for every possible change; that way clearly ends in stalemate. I agree with Dr Krugman; fiscal federalism is not a sensible way to go.

Dr Fujita

Thank you very much. Maybe we might have a short reaction from each one of the presenters. We start with Prof. Yu.

Dr Yu Yongding, Director, Institute of World Economics and Politics, Chinese Academy of Social Sciences

I think China and Japan and the rest of East Asian countries should think about the sustainability of the existing regional production networks. If we do not make some adjustment, this kind of trade pattern in trilateral embargos cannot be sustained for long.

I think one of the most important reasons for causing this kind of a situation is China's trade policy over the past 25 years. Because we adopted a policy of 'import in a big way and export in an even bigger way' in the early time of China's opening up. At the time we worried about the balance of foreign exchanges. So as long as we can export something abroad and we can maintain the balance of foreign exchanges, then we will not worry. Passing trade is supposed to be very good for this purpose because if you import something then we rely on the supplier of those passing components to export back to developed countries. I think now it is time for China to rethink this policy for supporting, encouraging, processing trade.

Second, Dr Krugman mentioned current account imbalance. I think the United States problem is very serious. United States debt over export ratio is as high as 300 per cent. As far as I know, the situation is worse than that of Brazil, something like 200 per cent. The United States is just better than Argentina at this moment. According to the predictions made by some investment banks, next year America's situation will be worse than Argentina's because Argentine's debt over export ratio will drop to below 70 per cent under the pressure of the International Monetary Fund (IMF). So definitely I do not think the huge current account deficit is sustainable for the United States; this is one side of the story.

Then we should think about our foreign exchange reserves because China now has more than US$510 billion foreign exchange reserves, and I think United States assets (federal bills and so on) is a very important component of this foreign exchange reserves. Japan's case is even more surprising; now that Japan has more than US$700 billion foreign exchange reserves. On the whole, we have more than US$1.3 trillion foreign exchange reserves in the two countries. If there is a big drop of the United States dollar, then how should we deal with this situation? I think the Japanese government and Chinese government should come together to talk about this, to address this problem. Is there any way out of this difficulty while reducing the risk and assessing the damage if there is a big drop in the United States dollar? On the other hand, we make the whole process more smooth avoiding making a disturbance to the capital market. I think we should come together to talk, and this will contribute to the momentum for regional economic integration.

Dr Fujita

Thank you very much. Prof. Kim, please.

Dr Young Han Kim, Associate Professor, Department of Economics, Sungkyunkwan University, Korea

First, I meant that with that terminology 'fiscal federalism', it is necessary to develop some kind of shock absorbing measures after we adopted a kind of East Asian integration. So we can say shock absorbing methods only for transition period after the reform subsequent to the integration. Whether there is a negative shock, even a politically unbearable shock really occurs to some participating country, we have to think about those kinds of measures which form a sustainable dynamic path for the economy. That is what I meant. So let us give up that terminology of 'fiscal federalism'. I will comply to your suggestion; I will not use that terminology any more.

Second, Prof. Venables mentioned that I used adverse words. I totally agree with you. There is a major source of gains from free trade, whether it is multilateral free trade or preferential free trade, in a reallocation of economic resources into a more efficient way. There is a real look at our economic resources to the sectors of comparative advantage. In this I totally agree, and that is what I learned from your textbook. What I am thinking about is that in the process of reallocation of economic resources there might be some possible side effects or distortion. We talked about trade diversion caused in the preferential trade agreement. Also, I think in the case of preferential trade agreement, not only trade diversion occurs but also some possible investment diversion occurs, and all those diversions might cause some kind of undesirable reallocation of economic resources. That is what we have to care about as a small open economy for example, Korea;

I think we have to specialize; we have to reallocate our economic resources to the sector of comparative advantages from the real global perspective, not a limited and restrictive regional context.

That is what I have tried to mention. So in that context I thought it would be necessary to minimize that kind of distorted reallocation of economic resources mainly due to the preferential trade agreement. But we have to try to figure out a way to reallocate our economic resources, almost like reallocating under a multilateral worldwide global free trade agreement. That is what I have mentioned.

Dr Fujita

Thank you very much. They seem to be agreeing in some parts. Let me call Dr Nidhiprabha.

Dr Nidhiprabha

Regarding trade diversion, usually the effect would be very large if the group has very large commutative barriers against non-members. So in that sense, if countries in the group follow multilateralism, trying to lower tariff rate at the same time, then the problem can be reduced. Actually, some of those fields that we have done follow that road.

In the case of Peru and Thailand, they are so far away from each other. Maybe in the case of Korea and Chile, they are so far away each other, too. But there are large Japanese communities in Peru. So that is why we try to get through into that market. We want to get some increasing returns. At the same time, we want to diversify the markets to reduce the exposure to some certain continent. Again, we are learning by doing, too. Actually we did it for the small countries. For smaller countries it is very easy to make a deal. There are not so many things to negotiate.

Now, about domino logic, I will put it this way: if the Philippines get tariff reduction from Japan, surely we lose a lot of market share to the Philippines because the processed food industry is highly price-elastic. That is what happened when the EU cut out Thailand's General System of Preferences (GSP) and we lost a lot of market share to other countries. The same is true for the case of the United States, which gives some preferences to countries in Latin America for helping them to suppress drug trade.

So in a way that is really sensitive; a small change in the tariff rate can put a lot of things out. My point is that whether all these ROE or tariff structures like that you need to have standardized, realize that there is some problem with the trade diversion. We should be cautious, but should have some standard.

Dr Fujita

Thank you very much. Let me conclude this session by my favorite metaphor using an article, titled 'Wrights' and wrongs of flight. It was almost 100 year ago when the Wright brothers flew in the air the first time in the history of humankind. That was a dream since the beginning of humankind that was finally realized in 1903. An interesting point about this article is what is meant by 'wrong'? Wrong means that in 1901, just three years before the first flight, one of the Wright brothers, I think Orville, proclaimed that it is impossible to fly, after 20 years of their struggling. He said, 'In the next 50 years, humankind will never fly; it is impossible to fly in the air for humankind in the next 50 years.' But, of course, just in two years, it happened; the test flight succeeded, and that is the 'wrong' part.

The important thing is to keep going, keep continuing the real effort, the full effort for the big dream. What does the big dream mean? Well, today we have the NAFTA area, the EU, and East Asia; these three areas have roughly the same total GDP. But in terms of population, we have about 2 billion people in East Asia alone, compared with EU's 450 million and NAFTA's 420 million. In that sense, East Asia has potentially much room to grow. But in order to achieve this potential, we really need the cooperation for integration in regional, sub-regional, and community level. Otherwise we are going to face a lot of trouble and stop at low-level FTAs.

I think we now know very clearly what the main issues are, including political issues. I think there are no insurmountable problems; we are getting very clear to what are the possible obstacles. That is why I think the important thing is people's communication and political reciprocity. Fortunately from next year we are supposed to have a real East Asian Summit, ASEAN+3. I am hoping to keep the momentum. There, I think, it is possible to make dream come true maybe in two years; maybe it takes a little bit more.

Let me show the next picture. That is the picture in 1907, four years after the first flight. That is one brother, maybe Orville, flying with a young lady sitting aside. After just four years, they are enjoying the flight. I think Japan and China are on the same airplane. The important point is that we are not in the big boat. In the big boat we can make some fight, but in the airplane the only way to survive is to become really tied up; a real community beyond the shortsighted and small issues. Of course some airplanes are flying higher, maybe like the EU. But we have a lot of room to go and I think the most important thing for East Asia is to keep going. I am very optimistic, and I hope many of you are optimistic, too.

Index